A Dictionary of
Foreign Words
and Phrases

A Dictionary of Foreign Words and Phrases

Tad Tuleja

ROBERT HALE · LONDON

© Tad Tuleja and Stonesong Press, Inc 1989
First published in Great Britain 1991
Paperback edition 2009

ISBN 978 0 7090 8956 8

Robert Hale Limited
Clerkenwell House
Clerkenwell Green
London EC1R 0HT

www.halebooks.com

The right of Tad Tuleja to be identified as author of this
work has been asserted by him in accordance
with the Copyright, Designs and Patents Act 1988

A catalogue record for this book is available from the British Library

10 9 8 7 6 5 4 3 2 1

Printed and bound by MPG Books Group, Bodmin and King's Lynn

For the most inspiring of
my many inspiring language teachers—

Dorothy Lange

Contents

Preface

The language of England is rich in foreign infusions. Thanks to the many invasions that have enlivened the history of that "right little, tight little" island, what we today know as English is far from the language of the Angles. A much changed, and still changing, potpourri, it echoes the world of the Romans and of the Franks, of fur-clad Gaels and raging Norsemen and archly opportunistic French barons.

It echoes, too, colonial times, when the English were on the giving end of invasions. From Shakespeare's day down to this century, the language has always profited from foreign contacts, as explorers and sea captains and merchant princes continued to swell the ancient word hoard with contributions from the Hindu Kush and the forests of the Wampanoags and New Spain.

Nor has the process stopped today. In the English-speaking world generally, and in the United States particularly, the mix of immigration and geopolitics, of electronic journalism and ethnicity, has continued to enrich the so-called King's English with snippets of Russian and Yiddish and even Sanskrit. As has been the case ever since the Romans' entry into Celtic Britain in the first century B.C., the Mother Tongue continues to prosper from foreign borrowings.

This dictionary acknowledges that debt, but in a manner that is circumscribed from two directions. I have tried to present here a selection of those foreign terms now used in English but that are neither on the one hand thoroughly Anglicized nor on the other merely pedantic.

Of the Anglicized words there are literally thousands. Indeed, the majority of foreign loanwords have by this time been so assimilated into mainstream idiom that they no longer announce their alien origins. Take the Latin word *compendium,* for instance, of which this book is an example; it was unknown to English folk until about the seventh century A.D. Or *blanch,* from the Old French for "white"; it didn't reach England until the fourteenth century. Or *ersatz,* a solid German term that only knocked on English shores during the First World War. Had I attempted to include all such adoptions, this book and I would have burst our mutual seams. For the lowdown on *compendium*—and on *status quo, hyperbole, siesta, avant-garde, rickshaw,* and *gauche*—the reader may profitably consult almost any standard English dictionary.

The "pedantic" was more difficult to excise because one person's *mot juste* is inevitably another one's *préciosité* and because I am no more adept than other lexicographers at screening out catchy entries simply on the grounds of obscurity. I have tried to focus chiefly on terms that are now common coin among literate English speakers but have also included many *rarae aves* because they were humorous, or instructive, or both. If I have erred in the direction of *terra incognita,* I plead a congenital fascination with the offbeat. *De gustibus non disputandum est.*

The preponderance of Latin and French is obvious and readily explained. Latin was the language of the educated in England throughout the long Middle Ages, and French picked up its fallen mantle from the Renaissance into our own time. Hence over 40 percent of my entries come from one of these two tongues. That percentage, I should point out, is much lower than you will find in the majority of foreign phrase books because I have made a concerted effort to cast a wide net: this dictionary contains fairly large offerings from the other Romance languages and from Yiddish and Greek.

The arrangement of entries is alphabetical. To make it easier to locate related items, I have included several Special Categories of entries beginning on page 133; these are indicated on the Contents page. An Index of Foreign Words and Phrases and a General Index follow the text, and internal cross-references are shown in SMALL CAPS.

My debt to printed sources is noted in the Bibliography. I also owe thanks to Marios Philippides for good counsel on the Greek; to Anthony Terrizzi, for the Italian; to my father and mother, for the Latin and the German; to Marion, for her enduring confidence and the Yiddish; to Adriana, for help with the ballet terms; and to *mi corazón* Andrée, for help with the Spanish and the phrase chart, and for being my anchor in all weather.

T. T.
Belchertown-Amherst

Pronunciation Guide

Instead of attempting to devise a pronunciation key that fully registered the nuances of the dozen or so languages represented in this book, I have aimed for phonetic approximations of the pronunciations in general use among literate English speakers today. The basic symbols used are as follows:

Vowels

a	a as in ash
ah	a as in father
ai	y as in why
au	ow as in how
aw	a as in tall
ay	ay as in play
ee	ee as in see
eh	e as in let
er	er as in mother
ih	i as in bit
oh	o as in go
oo	oo as in food
ooh	oo as in fool
oy	oy as in toy
uh	u as in but

Consonants

Consonants are pronounced as in English, generally; but notice the following special symbols:

ch	ch as in church
g	g as in gosh
j	j as in jar
k	k as in kayak
s	s as in soft
sh	sh as in shirt
th	th as in thin
zh	si as in vision

Since certain sounds in the European languages lack exact English equivalents, I also employ the specialized designations *oe, ue, eu, kh, 'r,* and the tilde (˜). These are explained below.

French. Borrowing a useful device from Mario Pei, I indicate nasalization by a tilde (˜) over the appropriate vowel. You pronounce a "tilde-ed" vowel as if you have a head cold: the spelling *ãh,* for example, comes out sounding something like simple *ah,* but with a nasal "hum" or "n" sound at the end.

The sounds of *ue* as in *rue* and *eu* as in *feu* are pronounced—or at least should be pronounced—as in French and not as, respectively, *oo* and *uh.* To say the French *ue,* place your lips into a pouty O shape and then attempt to say the vowel sound *ee.* For the French *eu,* aim for a midpoint between *eh* and *uh,* and throw in just the hint of an *r.*

The French *r* is uvular, meaning that it comes from high up in the throat. The designation '*r* in this book indicates the mere whisper of that uvularity, without a preceding vowel. Thus *être* is pronounced *EHT 'r,* rather than *EH-truh.*

German. The umlauted *ö* and *ü* are indicated respectively by the conventional transliterations *oe* and *ue.* To say the first, form your lips into an open O shape and then try to say *ee.* The German *ue* is the same as the French—or at least close enough so that only linguists can tell the difference.

The *kh* symbol has two distinct sounds. After the vowel *a,* it has a harsh, back-of-the-throat raspiness, suggesting the conventional, though erroneous, designation of German as the language of garglers; it also has this throat-clearing quality in Yiddish, as in *macher* and *chutzpah.* But when it follows an *i* or an *e,* it gives a softer sound, approximating English *sh.*

Spanish. The vowel sounds here, as in Italian, are regular and open. The *r* is trilled. I have opted for the Latin American pronunciation of *c* rather than the Iberian, because it is more commonly heard among English speakers. Thus a Spanish *c,* with or without the cedilla, is pronounced as an *s,* not as a *th.* My regrets to Thervantes.

Latin. Finally, and most problematically, the old nugget about how to do Latin. My high school Latin was the German variety, with a *w* sound for the *v,* a *k* for *c,* a *y* for *j,* a hard *g,* and a long *i* for the diphthong *ae.* Medieval, or church, Latin gives the *v* as a *v,* the *c* as an Italianate *ch,* the *g* and *j* both as soft, and the *ae* as a long *a.* I cannot settle the debate here and won't try. The approach I take is, I believe, a practical one; my guide is simply common usage.

This means that in most cases I have opted for an eclectic pronunciation, combining the Church doctors' *v* and long *a* with the ancient caesars' hard *k*. To give a notorious example, this gives *VAY-nee, VEE-dee, VEE-kee*—a historical impossibility which nonetheless is current idiom and which is also, if I may be forgiven this assault on semantic purism, more satisfying to the English ear than either the Roman *WEE-kee* or the softer, "churched" *VEE-chee*. For obscurer phrases, where there is no modern idiom, I have nodded toward the supposed "Roman" sounds. When Vergil anticipates better times, for example, he says not *joo-VAH-biht* but *yoo-WAH-biht*.

My apologies to those scholars who find this eclectic solution monstrous. I was no more comfortable hearing Vergil sounding like Dante than I was in speaking of genetic engineering as *"in WEE-troh"* fertilization.

For two stratagems I am particularly indebted to Eugene Ehrlich's wonderful little book *Amo, Amas, Amat and More*. I have retained his phonetic scheme for distinguishing the short and long Latin *o*: *HAW-mihn-nehm* and *DOH-lohr*. And, where the "good" Latin and the common English usage clearly diverge, I have given both the "proper" and the "idiomatic" pronunciations, with the latter shown second.

Stress is indicated by capitalization. Thus *MAHN-truh* is accented on the first syllable, *mahn-YAH-nuh* on the second.

Foreign Words and Phrases A to Z

A

Abendland *(AH-behnt-lahnt)* GERMAN: the West.

Literally this means "evening land," or the land where the sun goes down. Since the days of Spengler it has been used metonymically to stand for Western civilization. See UNTERGANG DES ABENDLANDES.

ab imo pectore *(ahb EE-moh PEHK-law-ray)* LATIN: sincerely, enthusiastically.

The literal meaning is "from the bottom of the breast." It sounds peculiar until you realize that to the Romans the breast *(pectus)* was the seat both of reason and of the emotions. So to speak *ab imo pectore* means the same thing as to speak from the bottom of one's heart. "Certainly Gorby is a charmer. But does he speak *ab imo pectore?*"

ab ovo usque ad mala *(ahb OH-voh OOHS-kway ahd MAH-luh)* LATIN: from the beginning to the end.

That is, thoroughly or without qualification, as in "Since the bass player was blind drunk, the performance was a shambles *ab ovo usque ad mala.*" The literal meaning is gustatory. *Ab ovo* means "from the egg" and *ad mala* "to the apples"—a reference to the most common appetizer and dessert of Roman meals. Used in this narrower, original sense, the phrase approximates our "soup to nuts."

absit invidia *(AHB-siht ihn-VIH-dee-ah)* LATIN: no offense intended.

Eugene Ehrlich is quite right to mention "the power that Romans attributed to animosity, whether or not openly expressed," and to suggest

3

that our "No offense" is a pale substitute for the Latin "Let there be no *invidia.*" *Invidia* is usually translated as "envy," but the original meaning of the verb *invidere,* according to my trusty Cassell's, is "to look upon with the evil eye." In Mediterranean culture, now as then, that is a more serious offense than mere envy.

absit omen *(AHB-siht OH-mehn)* LATIN: May it not be an omen.

Literally, "May the omen be absent." The expression suggests the extreme superstitiousness of the ancient Romans, who were wont to utter it self-protectively at the slimmest of provocations. Today, except for those who quail at black cats and broken mirrors, it seems less serviceable a charm. It can be used, however, as we use "God bless you" or *Gesundheit,* to offer *post hoc* protection to a sneezer. The Romans, who endorsed the common ancient belief that sneezing could presage danger or death, used it in just this way.

Achtung *(ahkh-TOOHNG)* GERMAN: attention.

Popularized by a host of stage Nazis of which probably the most recent, and certainly the most ridiculous, example was *Hogan's Heroes'* bumbling Colonel Klinck, this word means simply "Attention" or, in the military context, "Ten-HUT!"

acte gratuit *(AHKT grah-TWEE)* FRENCH: a free act.

"Free" in the sense of being unconditioned, having no discernible rational cause, being (to use the cognate) "gratuitous." A popular Existentialist IGNIS FATUUS; the prototype perhaps is Meursault's impetuous murder of an innocent Arab in Camus's 1942 novel *The Stranger.*

actus dei *(AHK-toohs DAY-ee)* LATIN: act of God.

Or, more literally and pungently, a "driving" or "moving forward" of God. Used in legal terminology to refer to such phenomena as whirlwinds, earthquakes, and falling trees. "I claimed the Porsche was fully insured, but they said the hailstones were a Goddamned *actus dei,* so I've got to replace the windshield myself."

ad astra per aspera *(ahd AH-strah pehr AHS-peh-rah)* LATIN: through hardships to the stars.

Narrowly *asper* (which gives us "asperity") means "rough," but the Romans used it broadly to mean "uneven," "harsh," "stormy," and "sour" (as in rough wine); Cicero even spoke of *tempora aspera,* which translates (roughly) as "tough times." The idea, then, behind the adage —which happens to be Kansas's motto—is a sound one: It'll be rough going, but we'll make it.

ad augusta per angusta *(ahd au-GOOHS-tah pehr ahn-GOOHS-tah)* LATIN: through difficulties to honors.

The message is the same as in the previous adage, but with an interesting, punning twist. Eugene Ehrlich, explaining that *"augusta* refers to holy places, *angusta* to narrow spaces," calls this a "fit motto for dieters."

ad captandum vulgus *(ahd kahp-TAHN-doohm VOOHL-goohs)* LATIN: to please or win over the people.

The verb *captare* gives us "captive" and "capture"; the root meaning is to seize, catch, or hunt down. It can also be used, however, to mean "entice" or "entrap," and this second sense gives us the idiom *ad captandum vulgus:* the classic example of "people capturing" was the Roman emperors' PANEM ET CIRCENSES. *Vulgus,* of course, gives us "vulgar," and it sometimes had this sense in ancient times: Latin authors spoke of the *vulgus* contemptuously, as we would speak of the rabble or the mob. Among contemporary ringmasters who perform *ad captandum vulgus,* one should number flag-waving politicians, romance novelists, the orangutans now running Hollywood, and 99 percent of Madison Avenue. Rupert Murdoch should adopt the expression as a motto.

ad eundem gradum *(ahd eh-OOHN-dehm GRAH-doohm)* LATIN: to the same degree.

Or, in the truncated version, *ad eundem.* The term has a specialized academic use, in that a university that wishes to honor the graduate of another university may confer a degree *ad eundem gradum,* without requiring the student to matriculate. Outside of the ivory tower, it's used more generically to suggest equivalency: "Partisans miss the point when they praise Gilbert over Sullivan or vice versa; the two men were geniuses not only symbiotically, but also *ad eundem gradum.*"

ad gustum *(ahd GOOHS-toohm)* LATIN: to taste.

As in "Add freshly ground coriander *ad gustum.*" Since this direction can be followed safely only by cooks who do not need it, it is a kind of culinary JEU D'ESPRIT, serving to keep the secrets of *haute cuisine* from the rabble.

ad hoc *(ahd HAWK; ad HAHK)* LATIN: formed for a specific purpose.

The literal meaning is "for this," and the sense is "for this purpose only." Used adverbially since the seventeenth century and adjectivally since the nineteenth, *ad hoc* typically evokes transience, often with a slightly negative connotation: "Let's solve this problem once and for all; we've had enough of your *ad hoc* solutions." But the expression is linguistically neutral, and to those who favor small victories over large promises, the connotation can be quite positive: Thomas Peters and Robert Waterman, in their book *In Search of Excellence,* praise the task forces of action-oriented corporations as effective examples of "adhocracy."

ad hominem *(ahd HAW-mih-nehm; ad HAH-mih-nehm)* LATIN: personal.

Literally, "to the man." In rhetoric an *ad hominem* argument attacks the defenders of an opposing position personally rather than sticking (see AD REM) to the point. The Gary Hart/Donna Rice fandango offers a perfect contrast of the two terms and simultaneously illustrates how easily a partisan can twist the term to his or her advantage. According to Mr. Hart, the press attacks on his probity were mere *ad hominem* smokescreens, having the sorry (and perhaps intended?) effect of distracting voters from the "issues." To the press, the candidate's honor *was* an issue: thus its sensationalist coverage was *ad rem.*

ad infinitum *(ahd ihn-fee-NEE-toohm)* LATIN: forever, endlessly.

Typically used adverbially to ridicule a long-winded monologuist, *ad infinitum* (abbreviated as *ad inf.*) may also describe any endless series:

"When you are waiting at a railroad crossing, the freight cars go on *ad infinitum.*" As a pedantic snap at garrulousness, it is often used interchangeably with AD NAUSEAM. The original Latin sense is "beyond limits."

ad interim *(ahd IHN-teh-rihm)* LATIN: in the meantime, meanwhile.

"I bought the stock on Thursday morning, intending to unload it on Monday. Lucky me: the market crashed *ad interim.*" Abbreviated as *ad int.*

ad kalendas graecas *(ahd kah-LEHN-dahs GRAI-kahs)* LATIN: never.

The first day of each Roman month was known as the *kalendae,* or "kalends," from which English gets "calendar." Greek reckoning had no such device, so that the Romans used the phrase *ad kalendas graecas,* or "on the Greek calends," to mean never. "We have got federal spending definitely under control and expect the deficit to be eliminated *ad kalendas graecas* or before."

ad libitum *(ahd LIH-bih-toohm)* LATIN: off the cuff; extemporaneously.

Better known in its abbreviated form, *ad lib,* the expression means "at pleasure" rather than by prearranged design. Since ad libs may or may not delight the audience, the pleasure referred to is that of the performer. There is an old joke about a dying atheist: "What will you do," asks a friend, "if it turns out there *is* a Hell?" "Simple," says the atheist. "Ad lib."

ad majorem dei gloriam *(ahd mah-YAW-rehm DAY-ee GLAW-ree-ahm)* LATIN: for the greater glory of God.

Abbreviated as A.M.D.G., this is the motto of the Jesuit order.

ad nauseam *(ahd NAW-see-ahm)* LATIN: endlessly.

"I'm as fond of Aruba as she is, but her home movies went on *ad nauseam.*" The sense of unendurable boredom which attends AD IN-FINITUM is even stronger in this expression, since the meaning is literally "to nausea." It's interesting to note that Latin *nausea* refers, originally, to seasickness. The word comes from the same root that gives us "navigation" and "naval."

adoxographi *(ah-DAWX-oh-GRAH-fee)* GREEK: trashy writing.

This is writing without *doxa,* or glory, that is, writing that would bring no fame or honor to its creator. It's an appropriate denunciation to level against the works of one's antagonists because, being obscure, it can be intimidating as well as rude. "It would be too kind to call this novel merely pedestrian. To me it is adoxographic twaddle."

ad rem *(ahd REHM)* LATIN: to the point; relevant.

Literally "to the thing," this is a rhetorical and legal term describing arguments that address the matter at hand, without oratorical tricks or red herrings. If Sergeant Joe Friday had been a Latinist, he would have asked his rambling witnesses to speak *"ad rem,* Ma'am, just *ad rem."* Compare AD HOMINEM.

advocatus diaboli *(ahd-vaw-KAH-toohs dee-AH-baw-lee)* LATIN: devil's advocate.

Generally used to describe someone who takes the unpopular side in an argument (either out of contentiousness or out of a zeal for the truth), this epithet originally applied to the Vatican official charged with finding objections to beatification or canonization—in lay terms, he argued against sainthood. Since the sixteenth century, this often maligned individual's title has been *promotor fidei* ("promoter of the faith"), and the *Catholic Encyclopedia* makes it clear that his function is a salutary one. "The seemingly negative work of the promoter of the faith undoubtedly has a great positive value, inasmuch as it prevents the Church from pronouncing a certain and favorable judgment on the life and works of a person without possessing unquestionable proof." Thus the misnamed devil's advocate helps to keep the hagiology pure; the devil, presumably, would like nothing better than to see it sullied by lax admission standards.

aere perennius *(AI-reh peh-REHN-nee-oohs)* LATIN: durable, lasting.

Perennis means "through the year" (from which our horticultural "perennial"), and *aes* is copper or bronze. In the Bronze Age, this metal represented permanence, since bronze tools were so much less brittle than the stone implements of earlier times. When a Roman spoke of something as being *aere perennius,* or "more durable than bronze," he meant (somewhat hyperbolically) that it would last forever.

aetatis; aetatis suae *(ai-TAH-tihs SOO-ai)* LATIN: aged; in the year of his or her age.

Both of these terms are truncations of the more proper *anno aetatis suae,* "in the year of his (or her) age." Frequently found abbreviated on old tombstones, it appears variously as A.A.S., A.S., and (most commonly) *aet.* When someone died in his or her eighty-seventh year, the marker might read "d. aet. 87" or "ob. aet. 87." See also NASCITUR, OBIIT.

affaire de coeur *(ah-FAYR duh KEUR)* FRENCH: love affair.

Literally "affair of the heart," the expression may echo the distinction in French classicism between fidelity *au coeur* (oh KEUR) and *au corps* (oh KOHR), or faithfulness of the heart and of the body. To Racine's contemporaries it was entirely possible to have one without the other, and modern Europeans may not be all that different: many men keep their wives in their hearts while blithely conducting *affaires de corps.* Ultimately the definition is purely personal: one person's roll in the hay may easily be another one's *affaire de coeur.* See also UN PETIT CINQ À SEPT.

affaire d'honneur *(ah-FAYR duh-NEUR)* FRENCH: an affair of honor.

In the days when the male sense of honor was even more puerilely sensitive than it is today, this was a code term for a duel.

aficionado *(ah-fee-see-oh-NAH-doh)* SPANISH: a fancier; a fanatic.

My Cassell's translates this as "amateur," which hardly does justice to its subtlety. An *aficionado* is a dilettante, but slightly batty: he or she has become inspired, captivated, utterly caught up in the trivialities of a particular mania. The classic case is Hemingway among the *toreros,* but one might also speak of Ronald Reagan as an *aficionado* of jelly beans, Paul Newman as an *aficionado* of racing cars. You may give up fortune and sacred honor for an *afición,* but (as Hemingway noted), you do not generally give up your life: that is the queer role of the professional.

a fortiori *(ah fawr-tee-OH-ree)* LATIN: all the more.

"Give your employees the opportunity to invest in the day-to-day workings of the plant—to have their voices heard on the line—and they will be eager, *a fortiori,* to invest in long-term corporate health." The French version is TANT MIEUX.

agent provocateur *(AH-zhāh proh-vah-cah-TEUR)* FRENCH: inside agent, one who "provokes" trouble.

Often equated with "spy," an *agent provocateur* is actually a very specific kind of spy: one who is planted within a subversive or politically antagonistic organization for the express purpose of leading it to the law. The classic modern example is the "narc," who enters a diffuse group of drug abusers to encourage their lawbreaking and then arrest them. The term also plays well in Robert Ludlum country.

agora *(AH-goh-rah)* GREEK: marketplace.

The usual appearance of this word is in the compound term *agoraphobia;* since ancient Greek markets were open plazas, a pathological fear of open spaces is known as *agoraphobia.* In general, it means the same thing as our "market." "These government subsidies are monstrosities; the sole determinant of prices should be the *agora.*"

al dente *(ahl DEHN-tay)* ITALIAN: chewy.

The traditional American fondness for overcooked food is giving way, in the age of nouvelle cuisine, to a European taste for crunchier fare.

Hence the current rage for chewy pasta, less-than-soggy zucchini, and other foods that are done *al dente,* or literally "to the tooth." This is slightly underdone by American standards, but not raw; if you break a molar on the lasagna, it's a bit too *al dente.*

alea jacta est *(AH-lay-ah YAHK-tah ehst)* LATIN: The die is cast.

The general meaning is "The decision has been made and cannot now be revoked." Julius Caesar was supposed to have uttered this common Roman saying after marching his army across the Rubicon River in 49 B.C., in defiance of a senatorial order; in using an expression from the argot of gambling, he was acknowledging the riskiness of his venture. Our expression "to cross the Rubicon"—meaning to take a decisive step into dangerous or unknown territory—also recalls Caesar's momentous action.

al fresco *(ahl FREHS-koh)* ITALIAN: open air.

Literally "in the fresh," meaning fresh air. A sign over a chic new Italian restaurant once announced, with great economy, "Al Bartelo's. Al dente. Al fresco." Meaning you could get the chewiest pasta in town on Al's terrace.

alieni generis *(ah-lee-AY-nee GEH-neh-rihs)* LATIN: of another kind.

The logical opposite of SUI GENERIS. Since the construction is in the genitive (possessive) case, it must technically accompany a possessing noun: *equus alieni generis,* for example, might be loosely translated as "horse of a different color."

alma mater *(AHL-mah MAH-tehr)* LATIN: one's university or college.

The association of this term with institutions of higher learning is over two centuries old: English satirist Alexander Pope made the connection in his 1728 masterpiece *The Dunciad.* But the literal meaning of the term is "nourishing mother," and it was originally applied to Roman goddesses—particularly Ceres, the grain goddess whose name gives us *cereal.*

als Adam grub und Eva spann *(ahls AH-dahm groob oohnt AY-vah shpahn)* GERMAN: when Adam dug and Eve spun.

From at least the fourteenth century, the image of Adam digging and Eve spinning was a popular representation of prelapsarian purity and particularly of the classlessness of Edenic "society." The radical English preacher John Ball, calling laborers to arms in the 1381 Peasants' Revolt, used as his text a coupleted version—"When Adam delved and Eve span, / who was then the gentleman?"—which referred clearly to the strife between rich and poor. Modern communarians, shunning religion as the opiate of the people, have ceased to make use of the proverb. (The sexual pun, incidentally—Adam delving with his "tool" and Eve "spanning" her legs—would have been perfectly obvious to Ball's audience.)

amicus curiae *(ah-MEE-koohs KOO-ree-ai; AH-mee-koohs KYOO-ree-ai)* LATIN: friend of the court.

One brought into a legal proceeding not as a direct witness to the case but to provide general advice and counsel regarding the social or legal issues involved. Technically an *amicus curiae* should be just that, a friend to the court alone; he or she should not be a party, even indirectly, to the dispute. I might, as president of the Sierra Club, appear as *amicus curiae* in a case involving toxic waste dumping; if the Sierra Club were itself suing the offending industry, however, my role would be that of litigant.

amicus humani generis *(ah-MEE-koohs hoo-MAH-nee GEH-neh-rihs)* LATIN: friend of the human race.

The Greek equivalent of this phrase gives us our word "philanthropist," from the Greek for "love" and "humanity." But because of the monetary connotations of that expression, it might be better to remember the Latin literally; certainly there are many *amici humani generis* who have never given a *sou* to the needy: the holy beggars of India, for example. The phrase reflects the same expansive attitude toward human possibility as is expressed in Terence's more famous motto, HOMO SUM; HUMANI NIL A ME ALIENUM PUTO.

amour propre   *(AH-moor PROHP'r)*   FRENCH: self-love, vanity.

"There is only one kind of love that truly satisfies the egoist, and that is *amour propre.*"

ancien régime   *(ĀH-see-ēh reh-ZHEEM)*   FRENCH: the old regime.

This term, which refers specifically to the monarchy that fell in the 1789 French Revolution, was popularized by Alexis de Tocqueville's unfinished history of that momentous event, *L'Ancien Régime et la Révolution* (1856). It might just as appropriately refer to any other supplanted governmental system: one can easily imagine a New Dealer speaking of the pre-Roosevelt era as an *ancien régime,* or a Reaganite tarring FDR with the same brush.

Angst   *(ahnxt)*   GERMAN: anxiety, psychological suffering.

Up until about World War I, *Angst* was a good old-fashioned German word meaning, simply, "fear" or "anxiety." Now, thanks to the combined efforts of the Freudians and the Sartre crowd, it has become an existential calling card: you can't really be "intellectual" or even AU COURANT these days unless you're carrying your fair share of *Angst*-baggage. The Yuppy Era has taken some of the shine off the concept, but it's still much too early to write it off: this *is* the Nuclear Age, after all. But one caution. If you intend to be fashionably *ängstlich* (that's pronounced *EHNX-tlik*) at a social gathering, you must remember to keep the misery vague: worrying about the Bomb doesn't make you *ängstlich.* The unknowability of its cause, in fact, is what makes *Angst* a much more impressive social disease than, say, herpes or hives.

anno domini   *(AH-noh DAW-mih-nee)*   LATIN: in the year of the Lord.

The Lord being, of course, Jesus of Nazareth, and the year being so-many-since-his-birth. The common abbreviation is A.D., which technically should appear before the date: A.D. 1641.

annus mirabilis *(AHN-noohs mee-RAH-bih-lihs)* LATIN: a marvelous year.

As Ehrlich remarks, this expression typically applies to "any year in which great events occur"—events such as public calamities or the birth of a cadre of famous figures: he cites 1809, for example, for giving us Darwin, Lincoln, Tennyson, Poe, and Mendelssohn. But each AFICIONADO will have a list of favorites. The fancier of Romantic poetry, for example, might choose the year 1798, for the Wordsworth/Coleridge joint venture *Lyrical Ballads*. The naval historian might pick 1942, for the turning of the tide in the Pacific. And the term is a natural for fake oenophiles. One can hear Basil Fawlty now: "Ah yes, 1929 was an indifferent year for most clarets, but it was an *annus mirabilis* for Bordeaux."

Anschluss *(AHN-shloohs)* GERMAN: union.

Generically *Anschluss* means "joining," but since March 12, 1938, it has been impossible to use the word that blandly. That was the day that Adolf Hitler, seeking *Lebensraum* in his native Austria, invaded and annexed that luckless nation. His term for this action was *Anschluss,* which stands right up there with *Pax Romana* as a euphemistic cloak for expansionism. When historians speak of *the* Anschluss, it's the 1938 event that they mean.

aperçu *(ah-pehr-SUE)* FRENCH: insight.

Like English "insight," this can cover a range of good perceptions, from the instant apprehension of cosmic connection (what Rennie Davis used to call "Astroflash") to the recognition that the "broken" television isn't plugged in. Its Gallicness makes it useful as a sarcastic pedant-goad; I know of no better way to deflate, say, an expert on the "new Finnish novel" than with a quietly withering *"Quel aperçu."*

à point *(a PWĀH)* FRENCH: done just right.

We are speaking of "done" as in steak. In Paris an entrecôte done *à point* is removed from the fire "at the point" of perfection or—to bring in the more general, nonculinary sense of the idiom—"just in the nick of time." To the French this means slightly rarer than most Americans are comfortable with. So too with the other designations of doneness.

What we would call "well done" is, to a Frenchman, impossible: there is no equivalent in his language. Our "medium" is his *bien cuit* ("well cooked"), our "medium rare" his *moyen cuit,* our "rare" what he calls *à point.* His rare is off our preference scale. A good thing, too: he calls it *bleu* ("blue").

a posteriori   *(ah PAW-steh-ree-OH-ree; ah POH-steer-ee-AW-ree)*
LATIN: inductive.

Inductive, or *a posteriori,* reasoning proceeds from the specific to the general: it draws conclusions about causes or general principles based on their supposed effect—literally "from what comes after." This empirically based type of reasoning, because it is prone to tendentious bias, has always been more popular than deduction: generalization flatters the generalizer as no true thinking ever can. If I see a Brazilian steal a car, reasoning *a posteriori* might allow me to reach many false conclusions; the most obvious might be "All Brazilians are car thieves" and "There are no cars in Brazil." Reasoning A PRIORI is much safer.

apparatchik   *(uh-pah-RAHT-chihk)*   RUSSIAN: party functionary.

Apparat means "apparatus," and specifically the bureaucratic machinery that runs—some would say "retards"—the Russian Communist Party. An *apparatchik* is a cog in that machinery. Our closest equivalents might be ward heelers—low-level members of the Establishment.

Après nous le déluge   *(ah-pray noo luh DEH-lyuezh)*   FRENCH:
After us, the deluge.

This quite percipient comment on what proved to be the penultimate generation of the ANCIEN RÉGIME is attributed to Madame de Pompadour, mistress of Louis XV and one of the most glittering lights of that doomed line. She died in 1764; her world followed twenty-five years later.

a priori   *(ah pree-OH-ree; ah pree-AW-ree)*   LATIN: deductive.

In philosophy, *a priori* reasoning works from the general to the particular: it deduces individual facts from principles that are already known—literally, "from the former." This type of reasoning underlies all Western logic, especially that embodied in the syllogism. If I know that (A) all Italian restaurants have checkered tablecloths and that (B) the trattoria Leonardo Machiavelli is an Italian restaurant, then I may safely conclude that (C) Leonardo Machiavelli has checkered tablecloths. I may be dead wrong in my assumptions, but my *a priori* deductions would still be sound. The great masters of *a priori* reasoning were Aristotle and Sherlock Holmes. Compare A POSTERIORI.

aqua vitae *(AH-kwah VEE-tai)* LATIN: water of life (whisky).

This is a fifteenth-century alchemical term referring, according to the *Oxford English Dictionary,* to "ardent spirits or unrectified alcohol." Why such spirits should have been linked to "life" is anybody's guess: mine are that they flared readily over heat, or that they imparted an ardent, albeit temporary, "liveliness" to the alchemists themselves. Both French and Gaelic preserve the conceit: the former with *eau de vie (oh duh VEE),* the latter with *uisce beatha;* both of these terms mean "water of life." The Gaelic, of course, gives us "whisky."

Arbeit macht frei *(AHR-bait mahkht FRAI)* GERMAN: Work will make you free.

A grotesque distortion of the Protestant ethic, this mendacious promise appeared on the front gate of the Nazi concentration camp at Auschwitz.

arbiter elegantiae *(AHR-bih-tehr eh-leh-GAHN-tee-ai)* LATIN: arbiter of taste or fashion.

Here's a thumbnail sketch of modern social history. In the seventeenth century, the *arbiter elegantiae* was Louis XIV. In Regency England, it was Beau Brummel. In America's Gilded Age, it was Mrs. Ward McAllister. Today it is *Women's Wear Daily.* Draw your own conclusions.

à rebours *(ah reh-BOOR)* FRENCH: against the grain.

The title of the quintessential decadent novel, J. K. Huysmans's 1884 story of a quest for ever more arcane and exquisite sensations. Huysmans has often been thought of as the French Oscar Wilde, and his hero, Des Esseintes, does share a certain deranged hunger for "experience" with Wilde's Dorian Gray. More generally, to be *à rebours* is to go against convention. "Are you reborn?" asked the evangelist. "No," replied the skeptic. "À rebours."

ariston metron   *(AH-rihs-tohn MEH-trohn)*   GREEK: the golden mean.

Literally this is "the best measure," but the sense in Greek is the same as that of Horace's more frequently quoted AUREA MEDIOCRITAS. *Aristos*, meaning "best," gives us "aristocrat" and "aristocracy"; *metron* gives us "metronome" and "metric."

arma virumque cano   *(AHR-mah vih-ROOHM-kway KAH-noh)*   LATIN: I sing of arms and the man

One of the most famous opening lines in all of world literature, this is Vergil announcing his theme: the story of the Trojan warrior Aeneas, the legendary founder of Rome. The full first sentence, translated, reads: "I sing of arms and the man who, exiled by Fate, first came from the shores of Troy to Italy and the coast of Lavinia." George Bernard Shaw borrowed the first two words for the title of his *Arms and the Man.*

arriviste   *(ah-rih-VEEST)*   FRENCH: social climber, upstart.

Why should this perfectly mundane word—literally it merely means "arriver"—have such unpleasant connotations? Because it indicates a person who has *just* arrived. An *arriviste* plus fifty years is Old Money.

ars gratia artis   *(ahrz GRAH-tee-ah AHR-tihs)*   LATIN: art for art's sake.

The "aesthetic" or "pure art" movement that flourished in France and England at the end of the nineteenth century adopted this phrase as a motto. In the ironically didactic texts of Walter Pater especially, it came to mean a devotion to stylistic brilliance and a disdain for the "social" uses of creative expression. The French symbolists entertained similar sentiments about *l'art pour l'art (lahr poor lahr).* The phrase survives popularly in America because it is the motto of M-G-M studios; one can feel Pater turning in his grave.

ars longa, vita brevis   *(ahrz LAWN-gah, VEE-tah BREH-vihs)*
LATIN: Art is long, life is short.

Coined by Hippocrates to suggest that the physician's art outlives the physician, this aphorism is often invoked today to remind us of the shortness of existence. Used by preening artists, it can reflect the self-congratulatory rather than sobering message that Art is the only thing that has value. Beethoven captured this sense perfectly when he was informed that his new, ninth symphony had not been well received. His reply was the artist's imperious "It will be."

así así   *(ah-SEE ah-SEE)*   SPANISH: so-so.

Literally, "like this, like that." Compare French COMME CI, COMME ÇA, Italian COSÌ COSÌ and MEZZA MEZZA.

au contraire   *(oh kohn-TRAYR)*   FRENCH: on the contrary.

A garden-variety Gallicism that has taken on a certain Hollywood panache because of its occasional appearance on the *Tonight Show.* Ed McMahon: "I bet that book contains *everything* you would *ever* want to know about modern etiquette." Johnny Carson: *"Au contraire,* my corpulent comrade . . ."

au courant   *(oh koo-RÃH)*   FRENCH: up-to-date.

The French expression *être au courant des nouvelles* means literally "to be in the current of new things" and figuratively to know the latest news. *Au courant,* as the kernel of that expression, approximates such American slang terms as "in the know," "with it," and the now obsolete "hip." One of the more amusing fusions of idiomatic genres I have encountered came from a New York high school student who had just spent a summer vacation in Paris. She spoke of her fashionable French companions as being "like, really, wicked *au courant."*

au dessus de la mêlée   *(oh DEH-soo duh lah MAY-lay)*   FRENCH: above the fray.

The fray here was the First World War; the term, which appeared first in a Swiss periodical, suggested detachment from the conflict. It might as easily be applied to those currently indifferent to LA LUCHA. The opposite would be *engagé (āh-gah-ZHAY),* or "committed" to political action.

au naturel *(oh nah-too-REHL)* FRENCH: as in nature.

The French use this term in the kitchen, referring to food that is plainly cooked—nouvelle cuisine is a modern example. In America and England, however, it is most often used as a euphemism for "naked," as in "The ecdysiast occasionally used veils but preferred to work *au naturel."* Used in this sense, the term displays a certain prelapsarian charm, implying that clothing, being a product of civilization, is somehow "unnatural," or fallen. Jean-Jacques Rousseau would have approved, obedient as he was to the eighteenth-century conceit that Nature and simplicity were inseparable. So too would nudists and figure painters—not to mention such giants of romanticist erudition as the writers of the *Playboy* philosophy *(sic).*

aurea mediocritas *(AU-ray-ah meh-dee-AW-crih-tahs)* LATIN: the golden mean, moderation.

Mediocritas means not mediocrity but a proper balance between two extremes. The Roman poet Horace suggested that this balance was the only protection against privation on the one hand and an EMBARRAS DE RICHESSES on the other. Ever since the appearance of the phrase in the second book of the poet's *Odes,* Horace has been known as a champion of the Golden Mean. Which led James Thurber to this erudite pun: "If you prefer COGITO ERGO SUM to the Golden Mean, you are putting Descartes before Horace." The Greek for this is ARISTON METRON, the Russian ZOLOTAYA SEREDINA.

ausgezeichnet *(aus-geh TSAIKH-neht)* GERMAN: excellent, outstanding.

I have loved this German adjective since I was twenty, and I include it here largely for nostalgia's sake—certainly it's not common in English. This is a pity, or as the Germans would say, *eine Schade,* for it has just the right touch of clipped exuberance to make it a worthy substitute for the currently popular teenism "awesome." It is spoken with heavy, exaggerated emphasis on the third syllable: "She finally asked you out? *Ausgezeichnet!"*

auto da fé *(AW-toh dah FAY)* PORTUGUESE: act of faith.

The English expression "act of faith" sounds pretty benign; the original *autos da fé* were anything but that. In medieval Spain and Portugal, an *auto da fé* was the Inquisition's official ceremony of interrogating, sentencing, and finally executing heretics: the most colorful features of this ceremony were the private torturing of suspects and their public burnings at the stake. It is these fiery executions to which the term more narrowly applies today.

autres temps, autres moeurs *(oh-truh TĀH, oh-truh MEUR)* FRENCH: other times, other customs.

This sounds like a rephrasing of Cicero's famous expletive *O tempora! O mores!* but it is really closer in spirit to St. Ambrose's famous advice to St. Augustine: When in Rome, do as the Romans do. The ethical limitations of this type of accommodationism are obvious, but in fairness to Ambrose it should be remembered that he was talking not about matters of life or limb, but about when and how long one should fast. Other times, other concerns.

Avanti *(ah-VAHN-tee)* ITALIAN: Advance! Forward!

Not as in "Advance and be recognized," but as in "Go on, you're doing great, keep going." In this sense the word is perhaps best known from the title of Mussolini's anthem "Avanti popoli," which might be translated roughly as "Forward with the People." More mundanely, *Avanti!* is also the polite command that you give when someone knocks on your door: it's like the French *Entrez,* the English "Come in."

ave atque vale *(AH-vay AHT-kway VAH-lay)* LATIN: hail and farewell.

Or, more mundanely, hello and goodbye. This combination of the standard Roman words for greeting and departure was immortalized by the poet Catullus in a valedictory to his dead brother. The Beatles used the same conventional formula, with certain lysergic alterations, in their hit song "Hello, Goodbye."

a vinculo matrimonii *(ah VIHN-kooh-loh mah-trih-MOH-nee-ee)* LATIN: from the bonds of marriage.

Said of a divorce. *Vinculum* means a cord or chain, and to be completely severed from the "tie that binds" is to be granted an absolute divorce. One might also speak, in a quite un-Roman manner, of being released from the bonds of good taste *(a vinculo gustus)* or even from the bonds of mortal life *(a vinculo mortalitatis)*.

ayatollah *(ai-uh-TOH-luh)* PERSIAN: sign of God.

The most highly respected leaders in the Shiite Muslim hierarchy are the IMAMS, but as the violent history of Iran since the Shah's departure has shown, you don't have to be an *imam* to get respect. *Ayatollah* is an honorific title accorded to religious leaders who are not *imams*. Khomeini is, as of this writing, PRIMUS INTER PARES among them.

B

baksheesh *(bahk-SHEESH)* PERSIAN: tip, gratuity.

"Tip" is the official, dictionary definition. In practice the line between tipping and bribery is often fuzzy, however, and in today's business circles, here and abroad, the term has acquired an unsavory tone: *baksheesh* is now "speed money" or "grease money"—that is, the "little extra" you extend to a business associate to shake the bugs out of a tricky transaction. Most American firms condemn the practice publicly, although there are probably very few fishing in international waters who do not encourage, or at least condone, it in private. In much of the world, *baksheesh* is, like its Mexican equivalent, MORDIDA, simply the way things are done.

ballon d'essai *(ba-lōh deh-SAI)* FRENCH: trial balloon.

Originally a balloon sent aloft to determine the direction of the wind, a *ballon d'essai* has, like its English equivalent, acquired extrameteorological connotations. "Their tender offer was too low to be genuine; I took it as a *ballon d'essai.*"

bambino *(bahm-BEE-noh)* ITALIAN: child.

This means both "little boy" and, more generally, "infant." Il Bambino is the Christ Child.

barrio *(BAH-ree-oh)* SPANISH: neighborhood, community.

Latins today speak proudly of *el barrio* as if it is both the generic Hispanic community and a state of mind. The technical meaning is simply "district" or "quarter": Barcelona's *barrio gótico,* for example, is the city's Gothic Quarter. In the American Southwest, according to the Vasquezes, *barrio* was once derogatory, meaning roughly "red light district." Given the historical links between prostitution and poverty, that is hardly surprising.

basta *(BAHS-tah)* ITALIAN AND SPANISH: enough.

In both languages this can be used quite in the same senses we use "enough": Italian *Basta latte,* for example, simply means "That's enough milk." But it often carries the sense of mock exasperation that, for example, a harried parent might use in telling her brood to shut up. In this frequent usage, it approximates our "Enough, already!"

bathos *(BAH-thohs)* GREEK: depth.

Literally "depth," but figuratively "dull" or "inane," generally to a ludicrous degree. Alexander Pope wrote a denunciation of his poetic rivals entitled *Peri Bathos, or the Art of Sinking in Poetry* which gives a good sense of its proper usage: the English equivalent might be "twaddle." The term has been unfairly conflated with *pathos,* which is something entirely different: the Greek *pathos,* like the Latin *passio,* means "suffering," and a pathetic work is one which depicts, or elicits, suffering. When a captious reviewer denounces a comic's "pathetic" attempts to be funny, what she really means is "bathetic."

beau geste *(boh ZHEST)* FRENCH: a grand gesture.

Literally a "beautiful deed," generally of a heroic nature and typically involving danger, or worse, to the doer. Sydney Carton's submission to the guillotine to save the lover of the woman he loves is a kind of prototype of the genre.

beau laid *(boh LAY)* FRENCH: beautiful ugly.

An oxymoron used to describe anything whose attractiveness, though undeniable, is at the same time an affront to aesthetic conventions: in my experience, Jean-Paul Belmondo and Charles Bronson have always garnered more than their share of the epithet. It may tie in with the common wisdom that, since "perfection" is unattainable, obvious blemishes heighten the effect of "close to perfection." This sentiment underlay the vogue for applied moles in seventeenth-century France; perhaps it also explains modern *haute couture.*

beau monde *(boh MOHND)* FRENCH: fashionable society.

Literally "the beautiful world," this refers not simply to the idle rich, but to that segment of their class which occupies itself with jets and soirees. A less frequently heard alternative is *haut monde,* or "the high world." Not to be confused with DEMI-MONDE.

bel esprit *(behl eh-SPREE)* FRENCH: wit, elegance.

Literally "beautiful spirit," *bel esprit* implies a certain airiness—a light-hearted but nevertheless profound intelligence. Noel Coward had it, and Oscar Wilde.

bella; che bella *(BEH-lah; kay BEH-lah)* ITALIAN: how nice; how pretty.

The standard street shark's comment (see PIROPO) at the passing of an attractive female, *Bella!* may also be used more generically, to approve anything eye-catching or interesting. "Maseratis leave me cold, but the new Lamborghini line—*che bella!*" The superlative, should you need it, is *bellissima (beh-LEE-see-mah).*

bella figura; brutta figura *(BEH-lah fih-GOO-rah; BROO-tah fih-GOO-rah)* ITALIAN: a good appearance; a poor appearance.

Basically these terms mean "a beautiful figure" and "an ugly figure," but they are used more broadly than in the simple aesthetic sense: Glendening explains that the figure here is generally one of social prestige, or "face." One sets out the good china to make a *bella figura;* one trims the lawn even when it doesn't need trimming to avoid cutting a *brutta figura.*

belle âme *(behl AHM)* FRENCH: a high-minded, lofty soul.

Literally "beautiful soul." This type was very big in the nineteenth century, when idealism was still respectable. The concept and the type have both fallen on hard times today: Mother Teresa may be the sole survivor.

benissimo *(beh-NEE-see-moh)* ITALIAN: excellent, great.

This is the superlative of *bene,* "good" or "well," and is used by the expansive Italians much more frequently than the simpler form.

ben trovato *(behn troh-VAH-toh)* ITALIAN: plausible, agreeable.

Literally "well found" or "well discovered," this refers to an expression that suits the situation with special finesse, a particularly arresting retort or turn of phrase. I've heard it used substantively, with humorous illogic, to suggest that Trovato was an Italian Joe Miller. "Bob couldn't carry a conversation in a bucket, but he sure knows his Benny Trovato."

bête noire *(beht NWAHR)* FRENCH: pet peeve, annoyance.

Literally this term means "black beast"—a rather scary image for something as minor as a pet peeve. Perhaps the original meaning was closer to the Greek NEMESIS: something that could undo, not just irritate, you. "I can put up with petit fours and caviar dip as well as the next person, but when they start cutting the crusts off the sandwiches—really, that's my *bête noire.*" The word may also apply to people. Anthony Burgess once referred to German-loving Madame de Staël as "Napoleon's *bête noire.*"

beurre sur les épinards *(beur suer lay-zeh-pee-NAHR)* FRENCH: a (financially) comfortable life.

The full French expression to describe something that increases one's financial security is *mettre du beurre sur les épinards,* literally "to put butter on the spinach." Only the French could come up with that image. I don't know whether the expression goes back this far, but according to Roy Andries de Groot's marvelous *Feasts for All Seasons,* the Gallic fondness for heavily buttered spinach may come from Brillat-Savarin. His recipe for spinach, borrowed from his local parish priest, called for three-quarters of a pound of butter to each pound of the greens.

bienséance *(bee-EHN-say-ÃHS)* French: decorum, good manners.

This means fundamentally the art of "seating well"—which shows you how important table seating arrangements were in courtly French society. Note that *séance* means "seat" or "sitting," which is what people do at a seance.

Bildungsroman *(BIHL-doohngs-roh-mahn)* German: "education novel."

Bildung means "education" not in a narrow pedagogical sense but in the broad sense of personal development. The classic German *Bildungsroman,* therefore, followed a protagonist through various stages of growth, to chart the development of character and mind. From Goethe to Thomas Mann, the Germans have been particularly enamored of the form, but they certainly don't have sole bragging rights: a superb ironic French example is the slim *Candide* and a definitive English one *David Copperfield.*

billet doux *(bih-yay DOO; bih-lay DOO)* French: love letter.

Billet (*bih-yay,* as the French pronounce it) usually means "ticket" or "bill," such as a train ticket or an invoice. When it's "sweet" *(doux),* however, it becomes a love letter. "I can't understand him," complained Roxanne, "His *billets doux* are so moving, but when he tries to speak he's so dull."

blaue Blume *(BLAU-uh BLOO-muh)* German: blue flower.

The dominant symbol of the German romantic movement, the blue flower first appears in Novalis's 1801 novel *Heinrich von Ofterdingen,* where it represents the object of that unspecified longing which gave the movement its febrile strength. A kind of Germanic IGNIS FATUUS, the blue flower can thus be used to stand for any vague and shadowy ideal. One yearns for it not with a bang but with a whimper; it signifies not so much a Faustian as a moping dissatisfaction. Having the "blaues" might be considered a toney German equivalent of "feeling blue."

Blitzkrieg *(BLIHTS-kreeg)* GERMAN: lightning war.

Hitler's invasion of Poland on September 1, 1939, was so rapid and effective that it was likened in the press to a bolt of lightning. This initial *Blitzkrieg* operation involved the use of dive bombers and tank divisions to penetrate the border, followed by motorized troop trucks to secure positions. Eventually *Blitzkrieg* came to mean any intense, rapid attack. What the British dolefully called *the* blitz ("the lightning") was the air bombing of London that began in 1940.

bon marché *(bōh mahr-SHAY)* FRENCH: inexpensive.

Literally "good price" or "good bargain."

bon mot *(bōh MOH)* FRENCH: witticism.

Literally "good word." "If she couldn't make you think, at least she would make you laugh: she had a *bon mot* ready for every occasion." Don't confuse this with MOT JUSTE.

bon vivant *(bōh vee-VÃH)* FRENCH: one of refined tastes and a lust for life.

This is a seventeenth-century term referring broadly to one who likes the finer things in life—what the Italians would call LA DOLCE VITA— and more precisely to a gourmand. The term actually says "good living," but it means the person who indulges in such living.

borracho *(boh-RAH-choh)* SPANISH: drunkard; drunk (n. and adj.).

This is common slang for a heavy drinker. Bentley suggests that it derives from *borracha,* for a leather wine bag.

borsanera *(bohr-sah-NAY-rah)* ITALIAN: black market.

The *Borsa Valori,* or simply *Borsa,* is the Italian stock market; *borsa-nera,* in Italian as in English, is the SUB ROSA version. Street hustler peddling stolen watches: "We're not talking Timex here, man. This is a genuine Borsanera."

bras d'honneur *(brah duh-NEUR)* FRENCH: arm of honor.

The literal meaning is broadly sarcastic, for the term refers to one of the commonest European insult gestures: the combination of an upward thrusted fist and a slapped bicep which, throughout the Mediterranean, means "Fuck you."

bricolage *(bree-koh-LAHZH)* FRENCH: contraption; something thrown together.

The verb *bricoler* means to putter about or tinker rather than stick seriously to a task: the productions of a *bricoleur,* therefore, are by definition jerry-built affairs. In an indictment of French anthropologist Claude Lévi-Strauss, David Maybury-Lewis once observed that when faced with ideas that he has insufficiently examined, Lévi-Strauss "simply piles on more ideas, till his whole enterprise looks less like a science than a piece of his own *bricolage.*"

Brünnhilde *(broohn-HIHL-duh)* GERMAN: Brunhild.

In Norse mythology, Brünnhilde was the leader of the Valkyries and the doomed lover of the hero Siegfried. She appears notably in Wagner's interminable opera *Der Ring des Nibelungen,* and because Wagnerian sopranos tend to be corpulent, the name has come to mean any large woman. "These mascaraed toothpicks don't do anything for me. Give me a woman with some flesh to her—a real Brünnhilde."

bubbe, bubbelah *(BOOH-bee; BOOH beh-luh)* YIDDISH: grandmother.

Although the strict meaning of *bubbe* is "grandmother" (from Slavic *baba*), in its various forms it is widely used today—especially on the Hollywood and Broadway circuits—as an all-purpose term of endearment: grandparents, grandchildren, other family members; spouses and lovers; even relatively casual business acquaintances—all may be heard addressing each other as "Bubbe." "Bubbelah" and "bubby," incidentally, are the marginally more informal variants of this already informal appellation. Whichever you use, it's important to get the initial vowel right. It's the same as the *oo* sound in "foot." Calling your Jewish friend your "dear booby," with the vowel sounding *oo* as in "food," will not win you points for cosmopolitanism.

bürgerlich *(BUER-ger-lihkh)* GERMAN: bourgeois.

Like its French equivalent, *bourgeois,* this means, broadly, "conventional and middle class" and, narrowly, "pertaining to the town": strictly speaking, *bürgerlich* values are those held by late medieval burghers, or town dwellers. What modern Marxists denounce as "bourgeois," Marx himself would have seen as *bürgerlich.*

C

caballero *(kah-bah-YEH-roh)* SPANISH: horseman.

Like "cavalier" in English and *chevalier* in French, this means basically one who rides a horse. Since in medieval times the only people wealthy enough to own horses were the aristocracy, all these terms took on the general meaning of "gentleman." Hence the phrase *muy caballero,* which, according to Bentley, "is occasionally heard as signifying the essence of gentlemanliness."

Ça m'est egal *(sah meht ay-GAHL)* FRENCH: It doesn't matter to me.

Literally "It's equal to me." Frequently heard in situations where someone is being asked to make a choice between indistinguishable options —or at least options that she considers so. "As for the Senate race, *ça m'est egal.* As far as I can tell, they're both fools."

camino real *(kah-MEE-noh ray-AHL)* SPANISH: royal road.

The everyday use means simply "highway," but the expression also carries the same idiomatic sense as our "royal road"—that is, the best or sure way to do something. "You want to know the *camino real* to financial success? Buy IBM in 1959."

campesino *(kahm-peh-SEE-noh)* SPANISH: country person, rustic.

This term, which is roughly equivalent to the Italian PAESANO or the English "peasant," was Ollie North's favorite description of the Nicaraguan Contras—and the people they were supposedly defending—during the 1987 Senate hearings on Irangate. The implication was that the Contras were simple folk, farmers at heart, and that the Sandinistas were urban villains. Compare FELLAHEEN.

Ça ne fait rien *(SAH nuh fay ree-EHN)* FRENCH: It doesn't matter.

Literally "It makes nothing," this phrase is used both to dismiss the importance of something said or done and—more commonly—to respond to a thanks. In usage it approximates "You're welcome." In connotation it suggests, "What I've done for you is so slight that it does not deserve your appreciation." Compare the Spanish DE NADA.

carpe diem *(KAHR-peh DEE-ehm)* LATIN: seize the day.

In other words, live it up now, because it may be the last chance you have. Horace offers this counsel in the first book of his *Odes,* following it with the reinforcing *quam minimum credula postero,* or "Put little trust in tomorrow." The idea has been put to good (or bad) use by centuries of philosophical hedonists, and it has always been one of the seducer's favorite ploys: quoting Horace makes you *seem* less a lecher. Saul Bellow used the thought, less lasciviously, as the title of his book *Seize the Day.*

carte blanche *(kahrt BLÄHSH)* FRENCH: a free hand, a blank check.

The term literally means "white card." Brewer suggests a plausible military origin. The white card was originally a blank sheet of paper which a victorious commander would force his defeated rival to sign; signing indicated that the loser acknowledged his surrender to be unconditional—that he agreed in advance to any terms that the victor might later write on the paper. Hence to give someone *carte blanche* is to allow him to do as he will. "When I gave you permission to receive their opening offer, it was a discretionary, not a *carte blanche,* power; what you've accepted is half of what we want."

Ça se sent, ça ne s'explique pas   *(sah seh-SÃH, sah nuh SAYX-pleek pah)*   FRENCH: One can feel it but not explain it.

An elegant variation on the old chestnut JE NE SAIS QUOI. Handy, as Beaudoin and Mattlin point out, when you have no clue what to say about the movie.

cause célèbre   *(kawz suh-LEHB'r)*   FRENCH: a celebrated case.

Any incident, typically a legal one, that generates wide popular interest. There is generally a whiff of scandal, crime, or at least notoriety about a *cause célèbre,* setting it apart from the mere news item. Thus *causes célèbres* are described as "incidents" and "affairs": Dreyfus, Patty Hearst, Lindbergh—that sort of thing. There is also a general understanding that such causes are created by the press. "What might have been a minor indiscretion on the candidate's part has become, thanks to the *Miami Herald,* a national *cause célèbre."*

causerie   *(kaw-suh-REE)*   FRENCH: chitchat, small talk.

From *causer,* "to chat," which is ultimately from Latin *causari,* "to plead a case." "I'm not very good at *causerie;* would you mind if we talked about Wittgenstein?"

Ça va   *(sah VAH)*   FRENCH: OK, all right, fine.

The literal meaning is "It's going," and the sense is "It's going all right." Informal and cordial at the same time, this is probably the most common "quick stroke" expression in conversations among French friends. Our formulaic "How ya doing?" "Not bad, how about you?" is generally condensed in Paris cafés to "Ça va?" "Ça va. Et toi?" A somewhat more active and less common equivalent is *Ça marche (sah MAHRSH),* meaning "It walks."

Ça va sans dire   *(sah VAH säh DEER)*   FRENCH: That goes without saying.

This has the same vaguely patronizing connotation—or at least potential connotation—as the English equivalent, because it implicitly conveys the idea that a previous comment was superfluous. "Hold the d'Yquem for dessert, you say? Well, *ça va sans dire."*

Ce que tu manges, ce que tu es *(suh kay too MĀHZH, suh kay too AY)* FRENCH: You are what you eat.

There would be no particular reason to cite this platitude in French rather than in English except that it originated in France, and from the pen of that nation's first great gourmet. He was Anthelme Brillat-Savarin (1755–1826), and his 1825 treatise *La Physiologie du Goût (The Physiology of Taste)* set the stage for his countrymen's characteristic delusion that they, and only they, know how to eat. The phrase given here is a condensation of his magisterial observation, *"Dis-moi ce que tu manges et je te dirai ce que tu es"* (Tell me what you eat and I will tell you what you are).

c'est-à-dire *(seht-ah-DEER)* FRENCH: that is to say.

An example of the French national tendency—one might almost call it an obsession—to explicate even the most obvious comment out to the *n*th degree. In my experience it is a much more common "filler" in Gallic conversation than "that is" is in English.

C'est la vie *(seh lah VEE)* FRENCH: That's life.

The most common Gallic resignation when events get beyond one's control. American equivalents include "That's just the way things go sometimes," "Shit like that's just gonna happen," and "Whaddya gonna do?"

ceteris paribus *(KAY-teh-rees PAH-rih-boohs; SEH-teh-rihs PAH-rih-boohs)* LATIN: other things being equal.

The simple function of this phrase is to act as a qualifying aside, but since in real life *ceteris* are seldom *paribus*, it can also serve to mask or even justify bias. *"Ceteris paribus,"* the apartheid enthusiast quipped, "all men should have equal rights. But our blacks cannot handle the responsibility." As George Orwell pointed out in *Animal Farm,* even in a state where all pigs are created equal, "some are more equal than others."

chazerai *(khah-zeh-RAI)* YIDDISH: anything worthless or disgusting.

Chazer in Hebrew means "pig," and the original meaning of *chazerai* is "pig stuff," that is, inedible food—inedible not because pigs eat it, but because pork is "unclean" for kosher Jews. By extension *chazerai* means anything dirty, cheap, or otherwise undesirable: poorly made merchandise, bad art, foul language. It has the same general sense as English "garbage," French *cochonnerie,* and Italian *porcheria*—the latter two of which might also be liberally translated as "pig stuff."

Cherchez la femme *(shehr-shay lah FÃHM)* FRENCH: Look for the woman.

An old proverb indicating the antiquity of the Gallic suspicion of women, even in the act of applauding them. It's used typically in the context of crime or at least social turmoil. The meaning is: When there has been some complication or trouble, look for a woman as the cause. Compare FEMME FATALE.

chez *(shay)* FRENCH: at the home of, at the place of.

Very commonly seen as part of the title of restaurants—the bistro Chez Patrice in Montmartre—this can also indicate a private residence. "Cocktails, 4 to 6, *chez* Jones."

chiaroscuro *(kee-ah-roh-SKOO-roh)* ITALIAN: light and dark.

This refers to a late Renaissance painting style emphasizing stark contrasts of illumination and shadow. The most famous practitioner was Rembrandt; the most impressive, Caravaggio. The term is translatable, with some caution, to other media: "The debaters were uneven, to say the least. They presented a *chiaroscuro* palette of wit and BATHOS."

chica; chico *(CHEE-kah; CHEE-koh)* SPANISH: girl, boy.

An affectionate diminutive, also used among adults with whom the speaker is familiar. *Chica* is also heard on the street as a very elementary PIROPO; it's not accidental that it sounds like English "chick."

chutzpah *(KHOOTS-pah)* YIDDISH: gall, arrogance, audacity, nerve.

Chutzpah is presumption of a particularly outrageous, and generally humorous, variety. People of all ethnic backgrounds display it, but its flavor is best suggested in Jewish anecdote. The "classic" definition, says Leo Rosten, is "the quality shown by the man who murders his mother and father, then asks the judge to forgive a poor orphan." The mugger who shouts for help as he is running away from his victim, the no-talent singer who books the Palladium, the marketing whiz who gave us the Pet Rock—all of these display varying degrees of *chutzpah.* My favorite example, though, is a personal one. When my friend Robert Lipton was at college, he was torturing a definition of efficient causality when his professor, losing patience, cut him off. "Have you actually *read* Aristotle, Mr. Lipton?" "No, sir," Bob said brightly, "but I've skimmed him."

les cinq lettres *(lay sank LEHT'r)* FRENCH: "the five letters."

This euphemism for *merde (mayrd),* meaning "shit," calls to mind our "four letter word." I have never heard it used in conversation and can only imagine it cropping up in circles where "Golly" is considered racy. If Bernadette of Lourdes stubbed her toe, perhaps *she* would shriek, "Oh, the five letters!"

cinquecènto *(CHEEN-kway-CHEHN-toh)* ITALIAN: the sixteenth century.

Literally "the 500," meaning the 1500s. In both art history and political history, *cinquecènto* means the High Renaissance; it's the age of Castiglione, Machiavelli, Leonardo, Michelangelo, and Raphael. Compare QUATTROCÈNTO.

claro *(KLAH-roh)* SPANISH: obviously, of course.

A common formula of agreement or sympathy. "I certainly wasn't going to pay him for a full day when he only arrived at 10:30." To that, *claro* would be an appropriate response.

Cogito ergo sum *(KOH-gee-toh EHR-goh SOOHM)* LATIN: I think, therefore I am.

This famous axiom was the starting point for French philosopher René Descartes's celebrated "philosophy of doubt," which led (inexorably, he believed) to a philosophy of certitude. Beginning from a position of complete skepticism, Descartes asked whether there was any single fact which human beings could know with absolute certainty—and concluded that thinking itself was this fact. For even in the act of doubting, a person thinks; and if the person thinks, he surely *is*.

From this premise Descartes constructed a massive philosophical edifice that has been generally forgotten. Outside of mathematical circles (where he is revered as the father of analytical geometry), Descartes is remembered largely for his opening line—just as Vergil is remembered for ARMA VIRUMQUE CANO, or Melville for "Call me Ishmael." That line, of course, has sprouted numerous tendrils, from the more-skeptical-than-thou "I think I think; therefore I think I am" to the tortuous but homier "I am; therefore I shop."

la comédie humaine *(lah KOH-meh-dee oo-MEHN)* FRENCH: the human comedy.

Applicable to the human situation at large, but deriving from the title that Balzac applied to his life's work, that vast array of social novels which portray every aspect of French life.

comme ci comme ça *(kohm SEE kohm SAH)* FRENCH: so-so.

Literally "like this, like that." Best uttered with a shrug of the shoulders or a slow wobbling of the hand. The meaning is that things could be better, but "I can't complain." "How have you been since the operation?" *"Comme ci comme ça."* Compare Spanish ASÍ ASÍ, Italian COSÌ COSÌ and MEZZA MEZZA.

commedia dell'arte *(koh-MEH-dee-ah dehl-AHR-tay)* ITALIAN: comedy of skill.

The dominant popular drama of Italy, and eventually all of Europe, from the late Renaissance on. Typically performed by traveling troupes, it involved extensive improvisation over skeletal plot outlines (hence the *arte* designation) and the use of masked stock characters, including such familiar figures as the braggart soldier Scaramouche, the particolored Harlequin, and the irascible, voracious Pulcinella—the prototype of Punch, from the somewhat later Punch and Judy shows.

comme il faut *(kohm ihl FOH)* FRENCH: proper.

Literally "as it should be." Something that is *comme il faut* is in line with the social proprieties. "Richard has an instinct for the right behavior. I have seen him with duchesses and with draymen; he has always been exactly *comme il faut.*"

compadre; compañero *(kohm-PAH-dray; kohm-pahn-YEH-roh)* SPANISH: companion, friend.

Common, and generally interchangeable, designations for close friendship: the Americanism might be "pal" or "buddy." *Compadre,* incidentally, also means "godfather."

condottiere *(kohn-doh-tee-EH-ray)* ITALIAN: leader, mercenary.

The cognate meaning is "conductor," but the original *condottieri* had nothing to do with either railroads or music. They were soldiers of fortune in the bloody, internecine Italian Renaissance; some, like the Sforza, attained noble rank through their depradations, while others remained hired lances. It is important to remember that true *condottieri* fight not for principles but for pay.

con mucho gusto *(kohn MOO-choh GOO-stoh)* SPANISH: gladly.

Literally "with great pleasure." A common formula for agreement. "Would you like to go to a movie tonight?" *"Con mucho gusto."* (Although this would be a bit formal for close friends.)

conoscenti *(koh-noh-SHEHN-tee)* ITALIAN: connoisseurs, experts.

Always plural, the *conoscenti* are literally "those in the know." What they're in the know *about* is not important: one can speak of the *conoscenti* of art, of music, of politics, or of letters (in which case they would be the *literati*). The singular, incidentally, is *conoscente.* So if your mechanic is a wizard with your carburetor, you might call him a *conoscente de meccanica*—although a simple *buon meccanico* would probably do.

cordon *(kohr-dōh)* FRENCH: string, rope, ribbon.

This noun gives us three useful expressions. A *cordon bleu (bleu)* is a "blue ribbon," which has the same general sense as in English and the special sense of blue-ribbon cooking; hence, for example, chicken *cordon bleu.* The *cordon rouge (roozh)* is that ring of Communist-run towns that surrounds (and, the timid say, threatens) Paris. And a *cordon sanitaire (sah-nee-TAYR)* is a line of isolation or quarantine. It has both a medical and a political use: the most famous *cordon sanitaire* of modern times is perhaps the Berlin Wall.

corpus delicti *(KAWR-poohs day-LIHK-tee; KAWR-poohs duh-LIHK-tai)* LATIN: evidence of a crime.

Because this means literally "the body of the crime," and because *corpus* sounds like "corpse," it's often assumed to refer to the body of a murder victim. That would be one kind of evidence, but not the only kind. In this situation, for example, a detective might discover a knife containing traces of a missing person's blood; that would certainly constitute enough of a "body" (of evidence) to conclude that a crime had been committed. No Latinist faced with this scenario would claim the detective lacked a *corpus delicti.*

cosa nostra *(KOH-sah NOHS-trah)* ITALIAN: the Mafia.

An Italian expression illustrating the insularity of Mafia shenanigans. It means literally "our thing." The sense is "our business," "our family," "our clan."

così così *(koh-SEE koh-SEE)* ITALIAN: so-so.

The commonest Italian expression of lukewarm enthusiasm. Equivalents include MEZZA MEZZA, ASÍ ASÍ, and COMME CI COMME ÇA.

così fan tutte *(KOH-see fahn TOO-teh)* ITALIAN: so do they all.

The "they" here is women. The underlying conceit of the Mozart opera by this name is that the fidelity of women cannot be trusted; what the female principals in Lorenzo da Ponte's libretto do is to betray their fiancés. The *opera buffa* was first performed in 1790; the implicit misogyny is timeless. Compare LA DONNA È MOBILE.

coup *(koo)* FRENCH: hit, strike, blow.

This gives numerous phrases in French, only a few of which have made it into English. A *coup d'état (day-TAH)* is a blow against the state, that is, an overnight ouster of its leaders. A *coup de grâce (duh GRAHS)*, or "blow of grace," is the death blow given to a suffering opponent. A *coup de main (duh MĒH)*, "blow of the hand," is a surprise attack. And a *coup de maître (duh MEHT'r)* is a master stroke. The Plains Indians used to "count coup" by coming so close to an enemy in battle that they were in danger of being killed, then touching him with a lance before escaping: each such touch—more hazardous in its way than a death strike—could be boasted of as one "coup."

credo quia absurdum *(KRAY-doh KWEE-ah ahb-SOOR-doohm)* LATIN: I believe it because it's absurd.

The most common variant of this odd maxim is *credo quia impossibile (ihm-paw-SEE-bih-leh)*, which in turn goes back to Church Father Tertullian's pronouncement, in his *Flesh of Christ*, "*Certum est, quia impossibile est*" (It's certain because it's impossible). The reconciliation of faith and reason has been a particularly knotty problem in Christian history, and Tertullian solves it here by ironic fiat. He was writing, it should be remembered, thirteen centuries before Copernicus.

cri de coeur *(kree duh KEUR)* FRENCH: a heartfelt cry.

Literally "cry of the heart." Compare the idiom *cri de conscience (kōh-see-ÃHS)* for "voice of conscience," and *dernier cri (DEHR-nee-ay)* for "the last word."

Cui bono? *(koo-ee BOH-noh)* LATIN: to whose benefit?

The cynic's question when attempting to determine the worth or worthlessness of a proposition. The idea is that there are vested interests behind anybody's support of anything, and discovering those interests is a step in the right direction to telling why someone votes A, B, or not at all. A homey English equivalent might be: "Whose bread is being buttered?" Particularly useful in ferreting out porkbarrelers in the midst of an election campaign.

Cuidado *(koo-ee-DAH-doh)* SPANISH: Watch out!

Or "Look out," "Be careful." This has the same usage as French *Attention* and German *Achtung:* the basic meaning is "Pay attention."

cum grano salis *(koohm GRAH-noh SAH-lihs)* LATIN: with a grain of salt.

The sense is the same in Latin as in English. The original meaning is probably that something that was hard to "swallow" by itself could be made more palatable if taken with a grain (or more) of salt.

D

da capo *(dah KAH-poh)* ITALIAN: from the beginning.

Abbreviated as D.C. in musical notation, *da capo* tells a performer to return to the beginning (the *capo,* or "head") of a piece and play it again. *Capo* is also the everyday Italian honorific for the head of a clan or organization: in Mario Puzo's *Godfather,* the ultimate Don was known as the *capo d'i tutti i capi,* or "chief of chiefs." Used in the mafiosi's sense, then, *da capo* might approximate EX CATHEDRA. "Who said to rub out the Tortellonis?" "The order came *dal capo* himself."

d'accord *(dah-KOHR)* FRENCH: all right; I agree.

Technically this means "I am in agreement with you," but its street usage is much more casual. The French use it ubiquitously in conversation, to cover everything from whole-hearted endorsement to a simple, offhand "uh huh"; allowing for Gallic formality, perhaps its closest analogue in English is "OK." I have engaged in hour-long "conversations" with garrulous Frenchmen using nothing but this term and a nod.

Das Ewig-Weibliche *(dahs EH-vihg VAI-blihkh-uh)* GERMAN: the eternal feminine.

Goethe's dominant symbol, in *Faust,* for that striving after perfection and experience that is the hallmark of the Faustian character. The idea appears at the end of the drama, in the line *"Das Ewig-Weibliche zieht uns hinan,"* or "The eternal feminine draws us on." The concept is a little more definitive and vibrant than the earlier romantic ideal, the BLAUE BLUME. It is not to be confused with the simply carnal "drawing on" that creates beauty pageants and singles bars. Goethe was no stranger to fleshly delights, but he was hardly so puerile as to make them the linchpin of his philosophy.

déclassé *(day-klah-SAY)* FRENCH: fallen in social standing.

Since the literal meaning is "unclassed" or "declassed," the implication is that the déclassé individual has had some social status—some "class" —to begin with. Thus the term is appropriately applied only to the shabby genteel: if the King and Duke in *Huckleberry Finn* really were a king and a duke, they would exemplify *personnages déclassés.* In democratic America, where status is typically confused with public prominence, commercial success, or simply wealth, the term may be applied more liberally to anyone who has made and lost a bundle, from fallen rock stars to bankrupt grocers. The hazards of such liberalization are clear: if anyone of fallen status can be déclassé, we may apply the term with perfect safety to such classless MACHERS as the Wall Street bunch led by Ivan Boesky. See also REDUCTIO AD ABSURDUM.

décolletage *(day-koh-leh-TAHZH)* FRENCH: a low-cut neckline.

Collet is old French for "collar." When fashionable French ladies starting doing away with collars around the beginning of the seventeenth century, they were literally performing *décolletage,* or "uncollaring." Today the term refers to bared shoulders, in general, but may include partially bared breasts.

de facto   *(day FAHK-toh; day FAK-toh)*   LATIN: in fact.

There would be no need for this legal tag if the law and reality were perfect partners. Because things which exist in law *(de jure [day YOO-ray])* don't always exist in fact—and vice versa—the distinction has attained the dignity of being Latinized. Homeowner who has just inadvertently allowed a thief to enter his home: "I know the law says you're not, but you're still *de facto* a trespasser."

déjà vu   *(day-zhah VUE)*   FRENCH: a sense of vague recollection.

The technical term for the sensation of "reliving" an experience is *paramnesia,* from the Greek for "alongside memory." The French equivalent literally means "already seen." It's less precise than the Greek, since such experiences often have tactile, olfactory, and auditory as well as visual components. But then precision isn't everything: you hardly get the appropriate eerie mystique out of "I have an overwhelming sense of paramnesia."

delirium tremens   *(deh-LEE-ree-oohm TREH-mehns)*   LATIN: alcohol withdrawal syndrome, "the shakes."

Delirium tremens is a physiological reaction to alcohol withdrawal characterized by agitation, hallucination, convulsions, and potentially death. The often humorously expressed abbreviation for this not at all humorous affliction is "the DTs."

demi-monde   *(DUH-mee-MOHND)*   FRENCH: the world of prostitution.

In contemporary usage, this term is quite sweeping: it refers to sex-for-sale in general, whether the venue is the Bowery or Park Avenue. Similarly, a *demi-mondaine* may be a streetwalker or a jetsetting call girl. But the original, Victorian connotation was narrower. The *demi-monde* was, in the guarded phrasing of my Webster's, "a class of women on the fringes of respectable society supported by wealthy lovers"—in other words, the ruling class's mistresses. Probably the expression *demi-monde* ("half world") arose because these women were half in, half out of the BEAU MONDE.

de nada   *(day NAH-dah)*   SPANISH: It's nothing.

Literally "of nothing." This is the Spanish "You're welcome." Like the French equivalents *de rien* ("of nothing") and *pas du tout* ("not at all"), it acknowledges appreciation by minimizing its importance.

deo favente; deo volente   *(DAY-oh fah-VEHN-teh; DAY-oh vaw-LEHN-teh)*   LATIN: God willing.

The verb *favere* means "to favor" or look kindly on; *vellere* means to wish or will. Thus both these phrases enlist divine assistance and are commonly used prophylactically, as English speakers use "Knock on wood." The idea is that, if you think things are going well, you should still cover your bets by thanking the Almighty: like the Spanish SI DIOS QUIERE, both terms are an insurance policy against misfortune. The most superstitious play it extra close by muttering both: *"deo favente, deo volente."*

deo gratias   *(DAY-oh GRAH-tee-ahs)*   LATIN: Thank God.

While *deo favente* and *deo volente* typically refer to enterprises that are not yet completed, this one refers to a FAIT ACCOMPLI: the situation that has turned out exactly as you wanted, and for which, *ergo,* you owe thanks. Before the touchdown play: "We'll connect on this pass, *deo volente."* After the completion: *"Deo gratias!"*

de profundis   *(day praw-FOOHN-dees)*   LATIN: out of the depths.

Today's *literati* know this phrase as the title of Oscar Wilde's last memoir, written while he was in prison for homosexuality. It is also the opening of Psalm 130—"Out of the depths have I cried to thee, O Lord" —used in Christian burial services.

de rigueur   *(duh rih-GEUR)*   FRENCH: compulsory.

Rigueur means "strictness" or "rigor." Something that is done "of rigor" is something that cannot *not* be done. "You know how I hate these private screenings. But Steven will be there, and the casting director. So I suppose attendance is *de rigueur."*

Der Mensch ist was er isst   *(dehr mehnsh ihst vahs ehr ihst)*
GERMAN: You are what you eat.

The German pun here *(ist–isst,* "is"–"eat") is lost in translation, but the line still serves as a concise expression of the materialist outlook. This is appropriate, for it was formulated by philosopher Ludwig Feuerbach (1804–72), a popular champion of "anti-idealism" whose 1841 critique of religion, *The Essence of Christianity,* strongly influenced the young Karl Marx. Compare the Gallic version CE QUE TU MANGES, CE QUE TU ES.

dernier cri   *(DEHR-nee-ay KREE)*   FRENCH: the last word, the latest style.

Literally "the last cry." "The geniuses told me last year that minis were going to be the *dernier cri.* Now I'm stuck with twenty gross of mid-thigh SHMATTAS."

los desaparecidos   *(lohs dehs-ah-PAH-reh-SEE-dohs)*   SPANISH: the "disappeared."

This is the journalistic euphemism to describe the hundreds, perhaps thousands, of political undesirables whom the Argentine junta spirited away, and almost certainly murdered, after its COUP D'ÉTAT against Isabel Perón in 1976. More generally the term describes any group of people whose whereabouts, for political purposes, is being concealed.

de trop   *(day TROH)*   FRENCH: too much, superfluous.

"It wasn't the most relaxing lawn party I've ever seen. I didn't mind the volleyball or even the croquet. But field hockey was just *de trop.*"

deus ex machina   *(DAY-oohs ehx MAH-kihn-nah; DAY-oohs ehx MAH-shih-nah)*   LATIN: the god from the machine.

The "god" here was a score-settling deity that Greek playwrights occasionally trotted out onto stage to untangle an otherwise unresolvable plot. The "machine" was a cranelike affair that hoisted the apparition out of the wings. From this we call any sudden providence or farfetched explanation, especially if unwarranted, a *deus ex machina.* Ishmael's coffin-raft, E.T.'s junk mélange transmitting device, Bobby Ewing's dream shower—these are classic (well, maybe not so classic) *dei ex machina.*

dinero *(dee-NAY-roh)* SPANISH: money.

This word probably entered Spain as the Arabic *dinar,* which in turn came from the Latin *denarius,* an ancient Roman silver coin.

Ding an sich *(DIHNG ahn ZIKH)* GERMAN: the thing in itself.

As opposed to the thing as perceived, or mediated, by human consciousness. This is a Kantian term expressing about the same reality as Plato's more celebrated doctrine of "forms"—that is, the reality beyond (distorting) experience. The nature of the distinction between reality and appearance is probably the oldest puzzle in philosophy, East or West, and Kant didn't so much unravel its complexities as give us a new jargon with which to juggle them.

dolce far niente *(DOHL-chay fahr nee-EHN-teh)* ITALIAN: sweet idleness.

Literally "sweet doing nothing." A term that seems to play best in the summer months, with a glass in one's hand. "This year we're taking the best of all possible vacations. Two chaise longues and *dolce far niente.*"

domani *(doh-MAH-nee)* ITALIAN: tomorrow.

This is less familiar to Americans than the Spanish *mañana,* but it has a similarly relaxed Mediterranean tone to it. Spoken to oneself as a kind of mantra, it's a good purgative for Type A behavior. "So I only drove 493 miles today. *Domani* is another day."

Doppelgänger *(DUH-pl-GEHNG-er)* GERMAN: double.

Literally "double goer" or "double walker," this term signifies a person's exact double, alive in the transcendent or spiritual realm. To the early German romantics, who were fascinated by the relationship between dreams and reality, the *Doppelgänger* was a favorite theme: Hoffmann and Heine both treated it, as did Joseph Conrad in his story "The Secret Sharer." The theme has been dormant for a couple of generations, but with the recent interest in "channeling" and metempsychosis, one may expect a rebirth. "By the way, Jim, I had lunch with your double the other day. He wanted me to tell you that you were Romulus and Remus in a previous lifetime."

Die Leiden des jungen Werthers *(dee LAI-dehn dehs YOOHNG-ehn VEHR-ters)* GERMAN: the sorrows of young Werther.

The title of Goethe's first major success, the 1774 short novel in which the artistic young hero, Werther, becomes so enmeshed in dreamy speculation and unrequited passion that he shoots himself as the only way out. Such was the state of adolescent Germany's soul at the time that a wave of suicides followed the book's publication. The mature Goethe dismissed the tale as juvenilia, but it remains a principal example of STURM UND DRANG, and of adolescent ANGST: Werther was a kind of Holden Caulfield without the humor.

Drachenfutter *(DRAKH-en-fooh-ter)* GERMAN: dragon food.

This literal meaning hints colorfully at the whimsically chauvinistic usage: the "dragon" here is one's wife, and the food or "fodder" is presents of flowers or candy that a bibulous husband might bring as peace offerings when he has stayed out too late.

Drang nach Osten *(DRAHNG nahkh AWS-tehn)* GERMAN: drive to the East.

From about the ninth century on, the Germanic peoples of northern Europe gradually migrated eastward and southward, penetrating Slavic-speaking areas and in general establishing cultural and political hege-mony. This slow, usually peaceful incursion, later labelled the *Drang nach Osten,* helped to breed the myth of "Aryan" superiority over the Slavs and also—to jump ahead a millennium—established the historical precedent for Hitler's more violent push to the East (and West) in the 1930s. The Nazi invasions of Poland and Russia in World War II were the culmination of a thousand-year "tradition." See also LEBENSRAUM.

dreck *(drehkh)* GERMAN AND YIDDISH: dirt, junk.

More pungent and impolite than CHAZERAI, Yiddish *dreck* means literally "dirt" but generally has the sense of something that ought to be thrown away: specifically, refuse or excrement. It's not often used to mean simply "dirt," as in "You've got some dirt on your face." The appropriate word for that would be *shmutz* (which in German means both "mud" and "smut"); the adjectival form is *shmutzig.*

Dulce et decorum est pro patria mori   *(DOOL-keh eht deh-KOH-roohm ehst proh PAH-tree-ah MAW-ree)*   LATIN: It is sweet and fitting to die for one's country.

Horace gives us this consolation for heroic sacrifice in his *Odes.* Wilfred Owen, the English poet who made that sacrifice himself a week before the World War I armistice, gave a bitter gloss to the observation in his poem "Dulce et Decorum Est," his most enduring lament about the slaughter.

Dummkopf   *(DOOHM-kohpf)*   GERMAN: a stupid person, a dolt.

The meaning of this cognate, "dumb head," is obvious enough, which is why it has been used AD NAUSEAM by stock stage "Chermans." It's a particularly fond appellation among "charming" Nazis berating their subordinates.

E

echt   *(ehkht)*   GERMAN: genuine, real.

As opposed to *ersatz* and KITSCH. There is no pretension about *echt:* it is true, unalloyed, straight from the shoulder. *Echt Haar,* for example, is un-Claireoled tresses; an *echt Picasso* is a real, not a forged, Picasso; *echte Farbe* are "fast," unbleeding colors; and a particularly satisfying performance of *Mother Courage* might be described as *echt Brecht.* This last is from Beaudoin and Mattlin, as is the description of shabby furnishings as, oxymoronically, *echt shlock.* (See SHLOCK.)

élan vital   *(ay-lahn vee-TAHL)*   FRENCH: vital force.

The philosopher Henri Bergson coined this term in 1907 to describe the unseen force he held responsible for evolution in human (and other animal) affairs. A simpler explanation than natural selection, at least. Dylan Thomas might have called it "the force that through the green fuse drives the flower."

Eloi, eloi, lama sabachthani?   *(eh-LOH-ee, eh-LOH-ee, LAH-mah sah-BAKH-thah-nee)*   ARAMAIC: My God, my God, why have you forsaken me?

In the Gospels of Matthew and Mark, Jesus' last recorded words from the cross. The other Gospels assign him less desperate utterances: "I thirst," "It is finished," and "Father, into your hands I commend my spirit."

el tenir y el no tenir   *(ehl tay-NEER ee ehl NOH tay-NEER)*   SPANISH: the haves and the have-nots.

The poor, as Jesus said, are always with us. This was certainly true in the 1600s, when Cervantes identified what he called the "two families" *(dos linages)* of the world: those who have and those who do not.

l'embarras de richesses   *(lahm-BAH-rah deh ree-SHESS)*   FRENCH: an embarrassment of riches.

A nice old expression illustrating the often forgotten truth that a surplus of success can be painful, if for no other reason than that it subjects one to solicitation and dire envy. "Embarrassment" is perhaps not quite right, though. The basic French meaning is "encumbrance," suggesting that the trouble with possessions is that they're *heavy.* This is what the shipwrecked miser found, of course, when he drowned because he would not let go of his gold. As Bette Midler once said, very sagely, to a talk show host: "Having it all can be a lot of trouble. If I ever get it all, I'm going to give some back."

éminence grise   *(eh-mee-nãhs GREEZ)*   FRENCH: gray eminence, power behind the throne.

James Rogers says that the original *éminence grise* was one François Leclerc du Tremblay, a.k.a. Père Joseph, a Capuchin monk thought to be an evil influence on Cardinal Richelieu during the reign of Louis XIII. Richelieu himself might be another choice, except that he was hardly as "gray," or in the shadows, as the term implies. "Forget the CEO; he's just a figurehead. The *éminence grise* in that company is the financial vice-president; get to him, and we've got the deal."

En boca cerrada no entran moscas *(ehn BOH-kah seh-RAH-dah noh EHN-trahn MOH-skas)* SPANISH: Keep your mouth shut and avoid trouble.

This is a marvelously pithy adage illustrating the value of a discriminating silence. The literal translation: "Flies don't enter a closed mouth."

encantado; enchanté *(EHN-kahn-TAH-doh; āh-SHĀH-tay)* SPANISH AND FRENCH: enchanted.

An old fashioned, and still formally acceptable, way of saying "I'm pleased to meet you." The idea in both languages is that the person to whom you have just been introduced is so arresting, in appearance or charisma, that you are under his or her spell.

enfant terrible *(ĀH-fāh teh-REE-bluh)* FRENCH: a prodigy, a boy or girl wonder.

Usually used in the same way as the German WUNDERKIND, this expression can also be more mundane and less laudatory: an *enfant terrible* can be, quite simply, a "terrible child," one who is obstreperous or unmanageable, especially in public. Steven Spielberg used to be spoken of, with veiled contempt, as the *enfant terrible* of Hollywood—a mantle he inherited from Orson Welles.

en passant *(āh pah-SĀH)* FRENCH: in passing, incidental.

Originally a technical term in chess, indicating the specialized "passing" capture of a pawn, this now refers to offhand, seemingly unimportant comments, which of course may be very important indeed. "His deposition was largely irrelevant. But a remark he made off the record and *en passant* gave me the exact clue I needed." Compare the Latin OBITER DICTUM.

entre nous *(ĀH-truh NOO)* FRENCH: confidentially.

Literally "between us," "between you and me." "I'll tell you every word the scheming bastard said, if you promise to keep it *entre nous.*"

épater le bourgeois *(AY-pah-tay luh boor-ZHWAH)* FRENCH: to shock the bourgeoisie.

Refers to activities that are embraced principally to get a rise out of middle-class, conventional people. If you paint your house chartreuse to annoy a neighbor, you are acting *épater le bourgeois*.

e pluribus unum *(ay PLOOR-ih-boohs OO-nuhm)* LATIN: from many, one.

In case you've never closely inspected a dollar bill, this expression appears on the banner that the eagle in the Great Seal of the United States (obverse side of the bill) holds in its teeth. The "many" are the original thirteen colonies, the "one" the union that they agree to form. The Civil War was fought, at great price, to see how this phrase should be interpreted.

Eppur si muove *(eh-POOR see moo-OH-veh)* ITALIAN: And yet it moves.

This is supposed to have been what Galileo uttered under his breath after the Inquisition had forced him to recant his dangerous doctrine that the earth moved around the sun. Useful, therefore, as a kind of verbalized crossing of the fingers, undoing what you have just said: "Her work has a shimmering abstractness that I find quite irresistible." (Aside: *"Eppur si muove."*)

esprit de corps *(ehs-PREE duh KOHR)* FRENCH: group spirit, team spirit.

This dates from the eighteenth century, when military units were beginning to develop that spit-and-polish clannishness that has characterized them ever since. *Esprit de corps* is not incidental to the effectiveness of a fighting (or sporting) group: indeed, it is that spirit itself—that elevation of braggadocio into a sense of honor—that makes both war and team sports possible.

esprit d'escalier *(ehs-PREE dehs-KAH-lee-ay)* FRENCH: a witty remark.

Not just any witty remark. The *escalier* here is a staircase, and the *esprit* that one displays in the expression actually only comes into play when it is too late to utter: a typical *esprit d'escalier* is the perfect squelch that you think of ten minutes after a rival has insulted you. The German equivalent is *Treppenwitz (TREH-pehn-vihts)*, which translates literally the same as the French: "stairway wit."

e tan e epi tas *(ay TAHN ay eh-pee TAHS)* GREEK: either with it or upon it.

Ancient Sparta, Athens's rival, was one of the most thoroughly militarized societies ever to grace the planet, and Spartan mothers evidently bought in to the ideal of toughness and valor no less fully than their constantly armored sons. At least that is the evidence of this catchphrase, which is supposed to have been the typical Spartan mother's farewell to a warrior about to do battle. The understood subject is the warrior's shield, so that the sense of the parting was this: Either come back carrying your shield or be carried back, dead, upon it.

Et tu, Brute? *(eht too BROO-tay)* LATIN: You too, Brutus?

According to Suetonius, these were Julius Caesar's last words, after he had been stabbed by a group of Roman senators including his longtime admirer Brutus. There were rumors throughout Caesar's later life that Brutus was his illegitimate son, and so this lament often appears as *Et tu, fili?* ("You too, son?") In Plutarch, the putative paternity is also clear: he gives the dying cry in Greek as *Kai su teknon?* ("You too, son?")

Eureka! *(yoo-REE-kah)* GREEK: I've found it!

This quite mundane expression has taken on a certain panache in Western culture because it is supposed to have been Archimedes' exclamation as he sat in a bathtub, some years ago, and discovered his eponymous principle of buoyancy. Because of this noble origin, it is generally reserved for moments of some import. But that is merely convention; the expression would serve just as well to announce the finding of the pickled oysters in a supermarket or the recovery of a lost set of keys.

ex cathedra   *(ehx KAH-teh-drah; ehx kah-THEE-druh)*   LATIN: from the chair.

The chair here is the chair of Peter: the papal throne in Rome. In Roman Catholic doctrine, when the pontiff pontificates officially (rather than, say, in an OBITER DICTUM) on matters of faith or morals, what he says is by definition infallible—in Church jargon, it's an *ex cathedra* statement. Notice the similarity to "cathedral." That's not accidental. A cathedral is the home, or "seat," of a bishop (such as the bishop of Rome); it is not, as is frequently supposed, merely a "big church."

As Ehrlich points out, this expression can also be applied, loosely, to any statements of true authority, religious or otherwise. "I forgive Nixon, really I do. When he announced that he wasn't a crook, he just wasn't speaking *ex cathedra.*"

exempli gratia   *(ehx-EHM-plee GRAH-tee-ah)*   LATIN: for example.

Abbreviated as *e.g.,* it means technically "for the sake of an example." Ehrlich raises a wise monition that this should not be—although it often is—confused with *i.e.,* for ID EST.

ex libris   *(ehx LIH-brees)*   LATIN: from the books (of).

A once common, now rare and pretentious, legend on bookplates. Technically it should be followed by the name of the book's owner in the genitive (possessive) case. *Ex libris John Kramer* doesn't work in Latin; the proper form is *ex libris Joannis Krameris.*

ex nihilo   *(ehx NIH-hih-loh)*   LATIN: out of nothing.

Lucretius proclaimed two millennia ago, *Ex nihilo nihil fit,* "Nothing is made from nothing." God and a few illusionists aside, the principle still seems sound today: for most of us, creating something *ex nihilo* seems as likely as forming it "of thin air." "He spoke well, I'll admit, but his argument for a solution to the trade deficit came strictly *ex nihilo.*" That is, it had no substance.

ex post facto *(ehx pawst FAHK-toh; ehx pohst FAK-toh)* LATIN: retroactive.

A law that is passed *ex post facto,* or "from what comes after," is designed to censure or punish actions that were not illegal at the time of passage. European monarchs have used the legal ploy throughout history to discredit or eliminate rivals, and because of this tainted past, *ex post facto* legislation is not permitted here: it is banned by Article I of the U.S. Constitution.

ex tempore *(ehx TEHM-paw-reh)* LATIN: extemporaneously; off the cuff.

Literally "from the time," presumably meaning the time of the actual presentation, rather than that usually devoted to preparation. "The keynote speaker was a fool. He had two pounds of notes and he still sounded like he was speaking *ex tempore.*"

F

fait accompli *(feht ah-kohm-PLEE)* FRENCH: an accomplished fact.

"There's no use arguing about whether or not we should buy the BMW. The *fait accompli* is in the driveway."

faute de mieux *(foh dah MYEU)* FRENCH: for want of something better.

For reasons that I do not fully understand, this expression always reminds me of Thomas Jefferson. It may have something to do with the Louisiana Purchase, but the more likely guess is Virginia. According to a hoary American legend, when asked what he would like on his tomb-stone, the aging Jefferson completely ignored his two terms as U.S. president; he wanted to be remembered, so he said, as the founder of the University of Virginia. So I think of this possible dying quip: "I would certainly prefer Monticello, but *faute de mieux* I'll take the White House."

faux pas *(foh PAH)* FRENCH: social blunder.

Literally "false step." See KLUTZ for some recent political examples. Idiomatic in English since the seventeenth century, this term is among the most widely recognized of our adopted Gallicisms. Those who are fond of giving thanks with the *faux français* witticism "Mercy buck-ups" torture this phrase into "foxpaw." Such humor draws a laugh in certain circles but is best avoided at state receptions.

felix culpa *(FAY-lihx KOOL-pah)* LATIN: the Fortunate Fall.

Literally "lucky" or "happy fault," this refers to the sin of Adam and Eve, which brought misery into the world but also paved the way for Jesus' Redemption. The fact that without their sin, there would have been no need for the Redemption—that most glorious event in Christian belief—is often spoken of as the *felix culpa*. C. S. Lewis analyzed the concept ably in his essay "Milton and the Paradox of the Fortunate Fall."

fellaheen *(feh-lah-HEEN)* ARABIC: peasants.

This is the plural of *fellah,* meaning "peasant." It's used occasionally in the Western press to describe the Afghani farmers-turned-soldiers fighting against the Red Army. Compare a similar use of CAMPESINO in Central America.

femme fatale *(fahm fah-TAHL)* FRENCH: an attractive, dangerous woman.

Literally "deadly woman." Keats enshrined the type, poetically speaking, in his "La Belle Dame Sans Merci" ("The Beautiful Lady without Mercy"), and it has been popularized in the movie era by vamp (vampire) Theda Bara, Marlene Dietrich, and a host of sloe-eyed, fast-on-the-trigger FILM NOIR heroines. But of course the implicit misogyny underlying the notion goes back to the beginnings of Western culture. In the pagan tradition the first examples were Homer's Sirens, who lured sailors to their death on the rocks. In the Judeo-Christian tradition, they were Lamia and, even more baldly, Mother Eve.

fiasco   *(fee-AHS-koh)*   ITALIAN: flask.

Why should "flask" mean "disaster"? It's an old glassblowers' term. If an apprentice glassblower fouled up the shaping of a vase or bottle, one solution would be to put utility ahead of aesthetics and redefine it as a simple container, or flask. "That's a very unusual vase, or ashtray, or bowl . . . what *is* that thing, anyway?" "That's my designer *fiasco.*"

film noir   *(feelm NWAHR)*   FRENCH: black film.

A style of movie popular in the late 1940s and the 1950s, characterized by urban landscapes, shadowed lighting, an aura of constant danger and mystery, and the presence, often, of FEMMES FATALES and hard-boiled private detectives. Highlights of the classic era include *The Maltese Falcon, The Big Sleep, This Gun for Hire, Double Indemnity,* and *Force of Evil.* Modern revivals of the genre have included *Chinatown* and *Body Heat.*

fin des haricots   *(fã day AH-ree-KOH)*   FRENCH: the last straw.

Literally "the end of the beans." "His style became more and more minimal until finally his canvasses were totally blank. A few fans hung on even then, but for most it was *la fin des haricots.*"

fin de siècle   *(fã duh see-EHK-luh)*   FRENCH: decadent, jaded.

This means "end of the century," meaning the nineteenth century originally, but unnervingly appropriate to this one as well. I cannot improve on Webster's excellent definition of the *fin-de-siècle* mood: a "literary and artistic climate of sophistication, world-weariness, and fashionable despair."

Fingerspitzengefühl   *(FING'r-SHPITS-ehn-guh-FUEL)*   GERMAN: intuition, "feeling."

Literally "fingertip feeling." It refers to the capacity some of us have for performing complicated tasks not by rote or by the numbers, but in a fluid, seat-of-the-pants fashion. Why the fingertips should have been chosen as the locus of this queer capacity is anyone's guess: perhaps it's a safecracker's metaphor. Hippie tax adviser: "The federal forms only take you so far. For creative returns, you need *Fingerspitzen-gefühl.* "

flagrante delicto   *(flah-GRAHN-teh day-LIHK-toh)*   LATIN: in the act.

Delictum here, as in the expression CORPUS DELICTI, means crime; *flagrante*'s original meaning was "burning." Hence someone caught *flagrante delicto* is discovered with his hand still in the cookie jar. Usually this means surprised in the midst of illicit sexual activity, but not always. In the Latin sense, a jaywalker can be just as "flagrant" as an adulterer.

folie à deux   *(foh-LEE ah DEU)*   FRENCH: a mutual madness.

Not simply two neurotic people living together, but a union in which each person's *folie* is enhanced and refined by the other person's. Readers of R. D. Laing will be familiar with the notion of madness as a social (and often familial), not an individual condition: a *folie à deux* is one example. The term is commonly used to describe the meshing neuroses of married couples (Scott and Zelda, for example), but it's also a good description of crime duos who cannot function apart. Leopold and Loeb, for example, or Clyde Barrow and Bonnie Parker.

folie de grandeur   *(foh-LEE duh grahn-DEUR)*   FRENCH: megalomania.

That is, intoxication with power. The classic French example is Napoleon, a more recent one Idi Amin. But any boardroom will give its own examples.

force majeure   *(fohrs mah-ZHEUR)*   FRENCH: irresistible force.

Sometimes any irresistible force, but usually—especially in legal terminology—the force associated with acts of God. See ACTUS DEI and the Italian equivalent of this term, UN CASO DI FORZA MAGGIORE.

Forsan et haec olim meminisse juvabit *(FAWR-sahn eht haik OH-lihm meh-mih-NIHS-seh yooh-WAH-biht)* LATIN: Maybe we'll laugh about this one day.

One of the great consolation lines in all literature. The exact translation is "Perhaps one day it will be pleasant to remember even these things." Vergil's hero Aeneas says this to his storm-tossed comrades in the first book of the *Aeneid,* after they are blown off course to North Africa. Among British schoolboys and other vestigial Latinists, it's still a celebrated enough line that you can get the effect of the full sentence by quoting just the first three words. "Rugby lost to Harrow again? At rugby? Well, *forsan et haec.*"

fress *(frehs)* YIDDISH: to eat.

In German, *fressen* usually refers to eating done by animals rather than humans; hence in Yiddish to "fress" has the sense of "devour" or "wolf down." You can have a little NOSH not a little *fress.*

frutti proibiti *(FROO-tee pro-EE-bih-tee)* ITALIAN: forbidden fruits.

According to an old Italian proverb, *Frutti proibiti* are *più dolci (POO-ee DOHL-chee)* or "Forbidden fruits are the sweetest." Possibly the ultimate reference is to the Garden of Eden story, but this "grass is greener" philosophy may also explain the appeal of married women to the lecher and that of shoplifted goods to the affluent teenager. Why, for that matter, would a million-dollar-a-year stockbroker want to engage in insider trading? Because of the lure of *frutti proibiti.*

G

gaudeamus igitur *(gau-day-AH-moohs IH-gih-toohr)* LATIN: therefore let us rejoice.

The opening words, and thus the title, of an old student drinking song, first sung by German undergraduates in the thirteenth century. The full first line is "Gaudeamus igitur, juvenes dum sumus" (Let us rejoice, therefore, while we are young). Obviously the priorities of college students haven't changed dramatically in 700 years.

gelt *(gehlt)* YIDDISH: money.

Gelt is an obvious variant of German *Geld,* which also means money and is pronounced *gelt.* Incidental but fruitful connections may also be drawn to the German verb *gelten,* meaning "to be worth," and the old English *gilt,* a form of "gilded." Playwright George S. Kaufman, according to Leo Rosten, once called his collaboration with Moss Hart a happy case of *"gelt* by association."

Gemeinschaft und Gesellschaft *(geh-MAIN-shahft oohnt geh-ZEHL-shahft)* GERMAN: kinship and association.

"Kinship" and "association" are rough translations. *Gemein* means "common" and *gesellen* "to join with." Thus *Gemeinschaft* is a type of social arrangement based chiefly on common interests and personal bonds; *Gesellschaft* is the more "advanced" arrangement based on formal political structures and legal alliances. The distinction between the two, while never absolute in human history, is a frequent theme of sociological writing.

Gemütlichkeit *(geh-MUET-lihkh-KAIT)* GERMAN: sociability, cosiness, a good atmosphere.

Gemüt in German has a range of meanings, from "mind" and "soul" to "feelings" and "disposition," all of them generally with a positive tone. *Gemütlich* thus means "sociable" or "good natured," and the noun *Gemütlichkeit* means the disposition possessed by, as well as the atmosphere typically surrounding, those of a *gemütlich* cast of mind. It's hard to translate this word precisely into a single English equivalent. Perhaps you will get the idea if I say that you find *Gemütlichkeit* in a loving family, a friendly tavern, an old-fashioned hayride. No matter how genial the clerk, you do not find it in a supermarket or at a tollbooth.

Gesamtkunstwerk *(geh-zahmt-KOOHNST-vehrk)* GERMAN: "total art work."

Richard Wagner's dream of an all-encompassing theatrical experience that would assault and/or satisfy all the senses. Opera, of course, always tended in this direction, but Wagner brought the operatic ideal—a lavish amalgam of the literary, the musical, and the artistic—to a kind of FIN-DE-SIÈCLE perfection by fusing the seventeenth-century French notion of spectacle into the horn-heavy nineteenth-century orchestra. Although they would no doubt be appalled to hear it, his aesthetic descendants in this regard include all those rock 'n' roll bands that rely on SON ET LUMIÈRE and smoke bombs to heighten the effect of their music.

gevalt *(geh-VAHLT)* YIDDISH: a cry of surprise, fear, or protest.

The German word *Gewalt* means "power," so that this Yiddishism seems to invoke "forces beyond." Often preceded by an *oy*, it's a more shocking and negative expletive than OY VEY, with the general sense, perhaps, of "Oh God!" It's what you might cry after totalling a new car, or when the dentist hits a nerve.

glasnost *(GLAHZ-nohst)* RUSSIAN: openness.

Russian dictionaries give this as "publicity," but etymologically it means something like "voice-ness." *Glas* is an old, poetic term meaning "voice" in an expansive, romantic sense. So for Mikhail Gorbachev to promise *glasnost* to the Soviet people means that he is encouraging them to find their own, true inner voices—and to speak them, fearlessly, in public. It remains to be seen, of course, how "open" this promise truly is.

gnothi seauton *(GNOH-thee say-aw-TOHN)* GREEK: Know your-self.

The most famous of the many inscriptions carved on the Temple of Delphi in ancient Greece, this is also frequently said to be the personal motto of Socrates. As such, it seems to counsel introspection—appropriate enough for the philosopher who claimed the unexamined life was not worth living. But the Delphic meaning is a little different. It's a warning to avoid overreaching, or what the Greeks would call HUBRIS. My *mentor hellenique,* Marios Phillipides, says that the best translation might be Dirty Harry's: "Punk, know your limitations."

gonif *(GAH-nihf)* YIDDISH: thief; clever person.

This can be used with either approval or disapproval, depending, I suppose, on how directly the *gonif*'s behavior has affected the speaker's own fortunes. One may admire the ingenuity of a little *gonif* who can do spreadsheets in his head at the age of twelve; if he later turns that skill toward embezzlement, he'll still be a *gonif,* but not so cute. An old expression says "You've got to have a little *gonif* in you to get ahead." But not too much.

Götterdämmerung *(GOE-ter-DEH-muh-roohng)* GERMAN: twilight of the gods.

Revelation 16:14–16 speaks of a dramatic final battle between the forces of good and evil, after which the world will be destroyed and a new, purified age begin. The place of the battle is Armageddon, which has therefore become a metaphor for mass destruction. The ancient Scandinavian equivalent of this battle was the so-called twilight of the gods, called Ragnarok. The German translation of Ragnarok is literally "twilight of the gods," or *Götterdämmerung,* which we remember because it is the title of the fourth opera in Wagner's mammoth tetralogy *The Ring of the Nibelung:* at the end of that work the entire world, including the high gods' VALHALLA, is destroyed by fire.

goy *(goy)* YIDDISH: a non-Jew, a gentile.

The Hebrew *goy* and the Latin *gens* (from which we get "gentile") both mean "nation." Rosten points out that in Biblical usage Israel itself was a *goy kadosh,* or "holy nation." Today, however, the sense is different: no Jew can be a *goy,* or vice versa. The plural of this common word is *goyim (goy-EEM).*

graffiti *(grah-FEE-tee)* ITALIAN: scratchings.

This is a variation of *sgraffiti,* which makes the cognate to "scratchings" a little clearer. The original graffiti, centuries old, were scratched into, not written on, clay walls. The singular, incidentally, is *graffito*—a word that is perhaps a little pretentious to apply to New York subway tags.

le grand peut-être *(luh grāh puh-TEHT'r)* FRENCH: the great perhaps.

Rabelais, on his deathbed, is supposed to have said, *"Je m'en vais chercher un grand peut-être"* (I go to seek the great perhaps). If true, it's one of the more sardonically honest of dying sayings, equivalent to Hobbes's "I am taking a fearful leap in the dark" and Henry Ward

Beecher's "Now comes the mystery." Browning translated it, in his *Bishop Blougram's Apology,* as "the grand Perhaps."

il gran rifiuto *(ihl grahn ree-fee-OO-toh)* ITALIAN: the great refusal.

The refusal of any high honor or public office. The prototype was Pope Celestine V's abdication of the papacy in 1294. Calvin Coolidge's decision in 1928, or LBJ's in 1968, might also be considered examples.

gringo *(GRIHN-goh)* SPANISH: an Anglo, a Yankee

The traditional, much disputed, etymology of this term is that it comes from a Robert Burns poem that contains the line "Green grow the rushes." Some say it is a corruption of *griego,* meaning "Greek," that is, "stranger"; others that it refers to the hated color of Black Jack Pershing's soldiers' uniforms: "Green, go home." At least the meaning is not in doubt. Once a blanket condemnation of all foreigners, today it means Mexico's northern neighbors.

gulag *(GOO-lahg)* RUSSIAN: the Soviet labor camp system.

Popularized by Alexander Solzhenitzen in his novel *The Gulag Archipelago, gulag* is an acronym for the Russian designation State Directorate of Corrective Labor Camps. The system of "reeducation" that has been carried on in the "archipelago" since Stalin's day is known in the West as "Siberia."

H

habeas corpus *(HAH-beh-ahs KAWR-poohs; HAY-bee-uhs KAWR-poohs)* LATIN: you are to have the body.

Until the mid-seventeenth century in England, accused persons could legally be imprisoned at the whim of the monarch or his ministers, and they could be kept confined indefinitely, without charges ever being preferred. It was to undo this parlous state of affairs that Parliament, in 1679, established the right to a writ of *habeas corpus* as a fundamental feature of English liberty. This writ was a judicial order requiring the appearance of an accused person in court, so that charges could be made and a defense mounted: the designation "you are to have the body" meant that the accusers—or the king's jailer—were to have the arrested person brought to court.

As part of its overall stand for due process, the U.S. Constitution specifically guarantees the right to *habeas corpus,* in Article I, Section 9, except in "Cases of Rebellion or Invasion," when "the public Safety may require it." Abraham Lincoln used that significant exception to suspend the right during the Civil War.

haiku *(HAI-koo)* JAPANESE: haiku.

A form perennially popular with budding poets, the *haiku* is a traditional Japanese verse genre consisting of seventeen syllables; as perfected by the seventeenth-century master Basho, it typically distills the fragility and beauty of the natural world in a single thoughtful image. An example from Basho: "A crow settles on a withered branch. Autumn dusk." And my favorite modern example, from the American lyricist Robert Hunter: "Ripple on still water, where there is no pebble tossed nor wind to blow."

hapax legomenon *(HAH-pahx leh-GOH-meh-nohn)* GREEK: a single occurrence.

Literally "once said," this refers to a word or phrase that appears only once in classical literature and whose meaning must therefore be devised from context. Most Greek examples are from Homer, but it is easy to imagine modern correlates: Poe's "tintinnabulation," perhaps, or Lewis Carroll's "borograves." In my family we also use the term to identify any sentence that is unlikely to have surfaced elsewhere before. Current front-runners include "He's aggressive in a nerdy sort of way" and "Who left the pepperoni in the egg tray?"

hara kiri *(hah-rah KEE-ree)* JAPANESE: ritual suicide.

Literally "belly cutting," this is the traditional method for a Japanese who has lost face or in some other way disgraced himself to put his troubles to an end. Since it involves disemboweling oneself with a samurai sword, it's not surprising that moderns shy away from it: the flamboyant and atavistic Yukio Mishima was one notable exception. Notice the correct pronunciation. Harry Carey—and his son Harry

Carey, Jr.—were actors, notably in John Ford Westerns; I doubt that either of them ever saw a samurai sword.

Heimweh *(HAIM-vay)* GERMAN: homesickness.

Constructed from *Heim,* "home," and *Weh,* "pain," this has the same sense as French *maladie du pays.*

hombre *(OHM-bray)* SPANISH: man.

In both its senses in English, to mean both the singular male and the generic human being. Best known perhaps from Western movies, where people like John Wayne and Clint Eastwood are continually being referred to as "one tough *hombre.*" See also MACHO, MACHISMO. It also appears often as an introductory filler, as we would use "boy" or "man." For this reason Gerrard and Heras Heras call it, somewhat excessively, "the most typical word in the Spanish colloquial vocabulary."

hoi polloi *(hoy poh-LOY)* GREEK: the masses.

Like the elitists who see him as a spiritual father, Plato uses this term contemptuously, as a contrast both to *aristos* ("the best") and to his own philosopher kings. It has the same sense as English "mob" or "rabble" and French *canaille,* although literally it means simply "the many." Notice that *hoi* in Greek is the definite article. Therefore, "I will have no truck with the *hoi polloi*" is not only snobbish but redundant.

homo lupus homini *(HAW-moh LOO-poohs HAW-mih-nee)* LATIN: Man is a wolf to man.

"Man" here means human beings, *homo sapiens,* and the "wolfishness" implied is the brutality and outright sadism so characteristic of our species in its weaker moments. A fair enough observation regarding us, but decidedly unfair to wolves, who are both more social and less rapacious than many humans.

Homo sum; humani nil a me alienum puto *(HAW-moh soohm; hoo-MAH-nee nihl ah meh ah-lee-AY-noohm POO-toh)* LATIN: I am a human being; I think of nothing human as alien to me.

The Roman playwright Terence gave us this majestically tolerant apothegm over 2000 years ago, and it has been a favorite of liberal educationists ever since: Cornell University, for example, has seen fit to emblazon it on the rafters of the student center, as a prod, no doubt, to undergraduate openmindedness. It's important to remember, however, that such a motto can also excuse indulgence, even vice. The Marquis de Sade, that much later explorer in the realm of human potential, would have found the concept quite congenial. Perhaps it is not incidental that the play in which Terence makes the remark is called *Heautontimorumenos,* or *The Self-Torturer.*

hora inglesa *(OH-rah ihn-GLAY-zah)* SPANISH: English time, Anglo time.

In Mexican and other Mediterranean-inspired cultures, time is very seldom of the essence; for most things, *mañana* is early enough. But with the gradual Coca-Colonization of the world, punctuality is growing in observation, if not exactly in popularity. To make it clear to her guests that they are expected to arrive more or less on time, a hostess will sometimes include this gentle reminder on an invitation: literally "English hour," it tells the recipient that an 8 P.M. soiree begins at 8 P.M. Without it, Mexican guests might arrive at ten. I know this from personal experience, since my wife and I once spent an amusing but frustrating afternoon—the entire afternoon—in a Yucatan theater waiting for the 2 P.M. show. Nobody else in the audience seemed a bit perturbed.

houri *(HOO-ree)* ARABIC: a beautiful woman.

A *houri* is one of the perpetually beautiful young women who are supposed to be "available" to the male faithful in the Muslim paradise. Given the androcentric bias of most surviving religions, it is perhaps not surprising that there is no equivalent treat for faithful females. (The phonemic similarity between *houri* and "whore" is purely accidental.)

hubris *(HYOO-brihs)* GREEK: pride, arrogance.

Hubris is far more serious than simple pride. It is the kind of pride shown by Julius Caesar when he accepted the chaplet reserved for Roman kings—an overweening self-confidence that implies, even if you do not publicly state it, that henceforth nothing can harm you. As the history of "royal" Caesar shows, the gods do not take kindly to such presumption, and typically the outcome of *hubris* is a serious, peremptory decline: that is why the Christian equivalent is "The pride which goeth before the fall." If you don't fall, perhaps it wasn't *hubris:* or, in the words of Dizzy Dean, "If you really done it, it ain't bragging."

In the Middle Ages, *hubris* meant "sin," and in modern Greek, it means "curse" in the blasphemous sense. Common to both these connotations is the sense of going beyond boundaries, of breaking the rule of MEDEN AGAN and so setting yourself up for retribution.

hysteron proteron *(HIHS-teh-rohn PROH-teh-rohn)* GREEK: the latter first.

A technical term in formal logic, this means the act of placing first an element that really should come later, that is, of confusing cause and effect. "The Ming vase broke into smithereens. I only grazed it as I walked by."

I

idée fixe *(IH-day FEEX)* FRENCH: fixed idea, obsession.

Not necessarily a crazy idea, just one that occupies someone continually. "For most physicists, as they get older, the possibility of finding a unified field theory becomes almost an *idée fixe.*"

id est *(ihd ehst)* LATIN: that is.

Abbreviated as *i.e.,* this is the commonest pedantic shorthand in scholarly writing. In speech you seldom hear the full term, but only the letters *i* and *e:* it comes out sounding like "Aieee!"

ignis fatuus   *(IHG-nihs FAH-too-oohs)*   LATIN: "foolish fire."

In the late Middle Ages, an *ignis fatuus* was an evanescent play of light that sometimes appeared above marshy ground, thought to be caused by natural gas combustion: among the common terms for the phenomenon were will o' the wisp and jack o'lantern. Because this fleeting spark sometimes frightened the timid or led the curious astray, it came to be a metaphor for any insubstantial dream or ideal. John Adams, in 1777, observed, "What an *ignis fatuus* this ambition is!" Compare BLAUE BLUME.

imam   *(EE-mahm)*   ARABIC: imam.

The critical difference between an *imam* and other religious leaders of the Shiite Muslims is that the *imam* claims direct descent from Mohammed. The term is also used, more demotically, to indicate the prayer leader of a mosque. See also AYATOLLAH, MULLAH.

immer schlimmer   *(IH-mer SHLIH-mer)*   GERMAN: going from bad to worse.

Literally "always worse." Best used, perhaps, as a dyspeptic gloss on Where the Human Race Is Going. "We can put nuclear missiles into space, we can explore the *Titanic,* but we can't talk face to face to each other. Is this Progress, or *immer schlimmer?*"

imprimatur   *(ihm-prih-MAH-toor)*   LATIN: let it be printed.

This word, appearing in the front matter of a religious book, signifies that its contents have been approved for publication by a bishop of the Roman Catholic church. A kind of positive holdover from the old, negative Index days, it provides pastors with a mechanism to protect the thinking of their flocks from contamination by un-Catholic sentiments. It may also be used more broadly, to suggest simple approval: "Running as a Bull Moose in 1912, Roosevelt sought no *imprimatur* from the Republican leadership." See also NIHIL OBSTAT.

infra dignitatem *(IHN-frah dihg-nih-TAH-tehm)* LATIN: beneath (someone's) dignity.

This already snobbish evaluation gains an added level of down-the-nose appeal by being virtually always seen in abbreviation—as if it is a code that only those who are above dignity know. "He invited me to the races but, my dear, that is so *infra dig.*"

In hoc signo vinces *(ihn hawk SIHG-noh WIHN-kays; ihn hawk SIHG-noh VIHN-chays)* LATIN: In this sign you will conquer.

The "sign" was a gigantic cross which the Roman emperor Constantine the Great was supposed to have seen in the sky, with this legend, just before his victory over his rival Maxentius in 312, outside of Rome. Whether or not he actually saw such a vision is open to dispute, what is clear is that, as emperor, Constantine adopted Christianity and thus dramatically transformed the cultural nature of the Empire.

in loco parentis *(ihn LAW-koh pah-REHN-tees)* LATIN: in place of a parent.

The commonest usage of this term is an academic one: the administration of a boarding school, a college or a university is said to act *in loco parentis* because it takes on many of the duties—tutelage, discipline, moral guidance—normally associated with parenting.

in medias res *(ihn MEH-dee-ahs RAYS)* LATIN: in the middle of things.

Long used by literary critics to describe works that begin, achronologically, in the middle of a story (Vergil's *Aeneid* is an early example), this term also applies more broadly to any social situation already in progress. "Giancarlo, SUBITO, please! You know I hate to arrive at Federico's parties *in medias res.*"

innamorata; innamorato *(ihn-ah-moh-RAH-tah; ihn-ah-moh-RAH-toh)* ITALIAN: lover, sweetheart.

The *a* ending is feminine, the *o* masculine. "He tells me he played poker until 3 A.M., but I smell an *innamorata.*"

in saecula saeculorum *(ihn SAI-koo-lah sai-koo-LOH-roohm; ihn SEH-kyoo-lah seh-kyoo-LOH-roohm)* LATIN: forever.

Saeculum technically means a generation, which the Romans estimated at 33⅓ years. Hence this expression means "into the generations of generations," or a very long time. It was a frequent tag in the old Latin liturgies to indicate the durability of God's designs.

In vino veritas *(ihn VEE-noh VAY-rih-tahs)* LATIN: There's truth in wine.

This proverb, which appears in Pliny's *Natural History,* refers to the propensity of many drunks to say whatever is on their mind, whether or not you want to hear it. It assumes a link between chattiness and veracity that, in my experience, is unevenly warranted: I have spent hours with bibulous comrades, listening to earnestly told bald-faced lies. Still, the observation has some truth. Alcohol does reveal *some* drinkers' souls; and it enables others to speak most bluntly while blaming the resulting FAUX PAS on their "condition." Given that so many drinkers lie, or remain silent, perhaps we should amend the observation: *In vino varietas.*

in vitro *(ihn VEE-troh)* LATIN: in a test tube.

Literally "in glass." Heard frequently these days with regard to genetic engineering, the term may be contrasted with *in vivo (ihn VEE-voh,* "in the flesh"), which refers to scientific experimentation performed not in the bottle but on living tissue. "Economic seers would have higher success rates if they performed their prognostications *in vivo* rather than in the Ivy Tower *vitrum.* The fundamental trouble with these geniuses is that none of them has ever met a payroll."

ipso facto *(ihp-soh FAHK-toh; ihp-soh FAK-toh)* LATIN: by that very fact.

The expression has somewhat the same sense as the English "by definition." "To the ancient Greeks, anyone who did not speak Greek was, *ipso facto,* a barbarian."

isvestyia *(ihz-VEHS-tee-ah)* RUSSIAN: news.

Or, in the usual context, *The News.* This is the name of one of the two large state-supervised newspapers in the Soviet Union, the other being PRAVDA (see PRAVDA).

J

Je ne sais quoi *(juh-nuh-say-KWAH)* FRENCH: I don't know what.

The commonest and still the best cop-out when you want to describe something that you can't. The sentence generally functions as a noun: "This wine has—how shall I say it?—a certain aromatic *je ne sais quoi* that I find charmingly impetuous." Compare the other great Gallic dodge, ÇA SE SENT.

jeu d'esprit *(JEU duh-SPREE)* FRENCH: puzzle, brain-teaser; witty comment.

Literally "game of the mind," this term can refer to anything from a particularly subtle BON MOT to more elaborate paradoxes and sophisticated conundrums. It doesn't refer simply to a tough problem, but always to one with some clever lightness about it. John Donne's *Catalogue of Rare Books Not for Sale*—a listing of nonexistent volumes—was a classic *jeu d'esprit.* So are the ingenious compendia of Richard Smullyan, the philosopher whose first swipe at popular logic was called *This Book Has No Title.*

jihad *(jee-hahd)* ARABIC: holy war.

It is one of the curious similarities between the Christian and Muslim faiths that they have both embraced the concept of the "just war." The last time the West was really blatant about this, in a religious sense, was during the medieval Crusades—although it certainly could be argued that the decimation of the American Indian and the general rape of the world by the British Empire were in their own ways modern *jihads.* Muslims remain blatant about it, even today. To many of them, especially Shiites, dying for Allah has become a sacred calling, and one of the more visible terrorist organizations in the Middle East styles itself, proudly, Islamic Jihad. Their philosophy is a Muslim version of "Kill for Christ."

joie de vivre   *(ZHWAH duh VEEV'r)*   FRENCH: joy of life.

Said of someone who is open to experience and, to substitute the English cliché for the French, "happy to be alive." A certain bubbliness attends the phrase, although that is perhaps incidental: you can have *joie de vivre* without being a Pollyanna. But being a Pollyanna doesn't hurt.

jus gentium   *(yoos GEHN-tee-oohm; joohs JEHN-tee-uhm)*   LATIN: international law.

Literally "the law of nations (or peoples)," this expression suggests a concord of opinion that has never existed outside legal chambers. The Latin term dates from the 1540s, when Europeans were just beginning to test how far their own provincialism could be "internationalized" by fire, book, and sword. Today the idea of one law for all peoples has pretty much gone the way of the dodo, and even the most avid internationalists are resigned to working on more tractable areas, such as maritime salvage and torture.

jus primae noctis   *(yoos PREE-mai NAWK-tihs)*   LATIN: right of the first night.

One of the more callous ingenuities of medieval law, the *jus primae noctis* gave a feudal lord the right to sleep with his vassal's new bride on the night immediately following the wedding. In many instances, this right was suspended in return for a payment of cash or kind—so it is difficult to say whether lucre or lubricity was the *primum mobile* behind the odd custom. The French called it *droit du seigneur,* or "the right of the lord."

jus sanguinis   *(yoos SAHN-gwih-nihs)*   LATIN: the right of blood.

This sounds gorier than it is. *Sanguis* here means the blood line. The reference is to citizenship rights: the *jus* is the right of a child, no matter where he or she is born, to inherit the citizenship of his or her parents.

K

kaddish *(KAH-dihsh)* YIDDISH AND ARAMAIC: "holy."

The *kaddish* is a prayer that closes most temple services and that is also recited for a year after someone dies, and on the anniversary of the death, by the relatives of the deceased. Because of this it is usually known as a "prayer for the dead," although it is not strictly speaking an elegy.

kamikaze *(kah-mih-KAH-zee)* JAPANESE: suicide, suicide mission.

Since World War II, when Japanese pilots went to glory by crash-diving · their planes into American warships, this word has spelled fanatical devotion devotion up to the point of death. Literally it means "divine wind": the wind that the young believers sailed on in their final BEAU GESTE for their divine Emperor.

karate *(kah-RAH-teh)* JAPANESE: empty hand.

Most authorities agree that what we today call *karate* was devised, around the fifteenth century, in Okinawa, by a people who had been prevented from carrying arms by their Japanese masters and who devised bare-handed and bare-footed fighting as a subtle recourse. The word comes from the Japanese *kara,* "hand," and *te,* "empty." Similarly, a *karateka* is a student *(ka)* of the art, and a *karategi,* or simply *gi,* is the uniform worn by such a person.

Katzenjammer *(KATS-ehn-YAM-er)* GERMAN: hangover.

Literally "the moaning of cats." The term may describe the type of sound that a hung over person would make, or the impression that noise would make on his sensitive brain. The Katzenjammer Kids were the mischievous young heroes of a long-running American comic strip; the name fit because their wild antics gave their elders headaches. Compare the interesting German idiom for listlessness or the blues, *moralischer Katzenjammer,* or "moral hangover."

ki *(kee)* JAPANESE: force, spirit, vital current.

Most Oriental spiritual disciplines, whether they are active and public like KARATE or more restrained and private like YOGA, include as a major part of their training the mastery and release of a vital "fluid" or "ether" or "current" as a way of achieving harmony with the cosmos. The yells that one hears in karate training, called *kiai,* are designed to release this unseen energy; the *pranayama* exercises of the yogi have the same fundamental purpose. *Ki* (Chinese *chi*) cannot be precisely defined in English; perhaps the closest Western guess would be Henri Bergson's ÉLAN VITAL, or the multilayered German *Geist.* However you choose to express it, the concept is central to spiritual progress: without *ki,* you are merely going through the motions.

kibbitz; kibbitzer *(KIH-bihts; KIH-bihts-er)* YIDDISH: to give unwanted advice; the giver of such advice.

The most frequently cited example of the *kibbitzer,* or person who *kibbitzes,* is the fellow who looks over your shoulder in a card game, giving a running commentary on your strategy; the backseat driver and the armchair quarterback also fit into the mold, as does anyone who is always ready with an opinion. The word comes, curiously, from the German *Kiebitz,* for a bird of the plover family called the lapwing. It is known in European folklore for its inquisitiveness and for what the *Oxford English Dictionary* calls a "thin, wailing cry"; one or both attributes must have given it a reputation for intrusiveness, which has passed eponymously to chatty humans.

Kibbitzer became popular in the United States, incidentally, after a struggling actor named Edward G. Robinson, né Emmanuel Goldenberg, enjoyed his first Broadway success in the Jo Swerling comedy *The Kibitzer.* That was in 1929—two years before he became Little Caesar.

Kinder, Kirche, Küche *(KIHN-der, KIHR-kuh, KUE-kuh)* GERMAN: children, church, kitchen.

This alliterative triad, which appears often in scholarly discussions of European culture, defines the parameters of the woman's role in traditional German society. It's hard to say it without a snicker now, but until very recently it was the norm. Compare the American macho notion that a woman's place is in the bedroom and in the kitchen—or the folk saying "barefoot and pregnant."

kishke(s) *(KIHSH-kuhs)* YIDDISH: stomach, "guts."

Usually, though not always, heard in the plural, *kishke* is from the Russian for "intestine." In Jewish cookery it is a baked sausage delicacy, but it is more generally used to mean the stomach, as in "No more, Ma, or I'll bust my *kishkes.*" To be hit, literally or figuratively, in the kishkes is to feel astounded or pained—as if you had been punched in the stomach. In this latter, and most common, sense the term approximates the pidgin Italian *labonza.* "Some traders anticipated Black Friday and got out in time, but many of them took it in the *kishkes.*"

kismet *(KIHZ-meht)* TURKISH: fate.

From the Arabic *qismah,* for "portion"—meaning one's share of life's ups and downs. Compare the Sanskrit notion of KARMA, the Greek of NEMESIS.

kitsch *(kihch)* GERMAN: trash

In German the noun *Kitsch* means "trash" or "trumpery," and the adjective *kitschig* means "trashy." In English the noun form serves both purposes, and usually in the context of "art talk." Susan Sontag popularized the word in the 1960s with her celebrated essay on the related phenomenon of "camp," but Germans had been applying it long before that to both sentimental drama and tawdry ornament. An excess of cheap decoration, a too obvious pulling of the heartstrings, a general absence of subtlety—these are the attributes of *kitsch.* Erich Segal's *Love Story* was once spoken of as the *kitsch* novel par excellence; Thomas Keene (he of the big-eyed urchins) is a major *Kitschmeister* of the art world; and Miami's Fontainebleau Hotel, according to Beaudoin and Mattlin, is the *kitsch* architect's unrivalled "Parthenon."

klutz *(kluhts)* YIDDISH: a clumsy, stupid, or insensitive person.

The *klutz* belongs to the same loser clan as the NEBBISH and the SHLEMIHL, but his failings are often more blatant. The German noun *Klotz* means "log" or "block of wood," and by extension a bungler or blockhead. Yiddish retains the extended connotation and uses it, as does German, to indicate clumsiness of expression as well as action. The *klutz* can put his foot in it literally by breaking china or dancing on a partner's toes. But he can also do so figuratively—as politicians continually discover to their chagrin, even at the highest levels of public life.

An honor roll of recent presidential-level klutziness, for example, would include Jesse Jackson's characterization of New York City as "Hymietown"; Jimmy Carter's confession to a *Playboy* cleric that he had committed adultery "in his heart"; Gary Hart's smiling for the camera with Donna Rice perched upon his knee; Ronald Reagan's announcement to the nation that his administration had "never—I repeat, never —traded arms for hostages"; and last (but certainly not least) Gerald "Surefoot" Ford's observation that Eastern Europe was not under Soviet domination.

koan *(KOH-uhn)* JAPANESE: koan.

Frequently translated as "puzzle" or "paradox," this actually means "public proposition." It's a pithy, usually poetic statement presented to a Zen student by his or her teacher and meant to serve as a spur to enlightenment. The most famous example in the West is the quizzical observation "What is the sound of one hand clapping?" Students meditate on *koans* to achieve insight into the nature of reality—not to find the "right answer." In Zen study there is no right answer.

kogda rak svisnet *(KOHG-dah rahk SVIHZ-neht)* RUSSIAN: never.

Literally "when the crayfish whistles." Equivalent to our "when hell freezes over" or "when pigs fly." An appropriate dirk for those Russophobes who have gotten tired of the conventional saber rattling: "Of course GLASNOST will make a big difference. *Kogda rak svisnet,* I mean."

koinos topos *(KOH-ee-nohs TOH-pohs)* GREEK: the given wisdom, commonplace.

Literally "common place," and used in the sense of "common topic" to refer to any trite saying or idea. "It may be true that Big Business is only interested in the bottom line; it's also, quite blatantly, a *koinos topos.*"

kusat sebe lokti *(KOO-saht seh-beh LOHK-tee)* RUSSIAN: to cry over spilt milk.

That is, to perform an action that is both retributive and useless. The literal meaning is "to bite one's elbows."

kvetsch *(kvehch)* YIDDISH: to complain; one who complains constantly.

Derived from the German verb *quetschen,* "to squeeze," the Yiddish retains this original sense and adds several of its own. Leo Rosten says that as a verb, *kvetsch* can mean (in addition to "squeeze"), "fuss," "complain," "delay," "shrug," and "eke out a living"; while as a noun —also seen as *kvetscher*—it may mean a constant griper, an inefficient worker, or a "wet blanket." By far the commonest usage refers to carping, nit-picking, or general bitchiness. Naturally the attribution is subjective, so that one person's reasonable objection is seen by another as mere kvetching. Rosten, for example, mentions a lapel button that deflates the brittle intelligence of one twentieth-century literary hero in four words: "Kafka was a kvetch." I have heard the same sentiment about Schopenhauer.

L

la dolce vita *(lah DOHL-cheh VEE-tah)* ITALIAN: the sweet life.

In Fellini's 1960 film, *dolce* meant rich, randy, bored, and booze-sodden. In the Yuppy Era, the closest approximation might be the cant ideal "having it all."

La donna è mobile *(lah DOH-nah eh MOH-bee-lay)* ITALIAN: Women are fickle.

An expression of the same male suspiciousness as that which animates *Così Fan Tutte,* this is the title of an aria from Verdi's 1851 opera *Rigoletto.* A showpiece for tenors, it is sung in broad self-justification by the philandering Duke of Mantua.

Laisser les bons temps rouler   *(LEH-zay lay BŌH tãhm roo-LAY)*
FRENCH: Let the good times roll.

This is Cajun French, pirating an Americanism that is still heard in the lyrics of many blues songs. Cajun musicians use it too, with their characteristic "Looziana" zip. If you're speaking to Cajuns, don't pronounce this as if you were in Paris: Cajun French is more relaxed and good-humored. If a French teacher tells you you're saying it right, you're not.

la lucha   *(lah LOO-chah)*   SPANISH: the struggle.

In internationalist-minded leftist circles there is only one struggle: the fight for the oppressed of the planet to free themselves from the chains of capitalism. Because of the Spanish influence here, American leftists sometimes call this *la lucha;* in France, the equivalent term is *la lutte (lah LUET).* To be part of *la lutte* is to be what the French call *engagé,* "engaged." Not to be part of it is to be what Stokeley Carmichael called "part of the problem." See AU DESSUS DE LA MÊLÉE.

landsman   *(LAHNTS-mahn)*   YIDDISH: fellow countryman.

Identical to the German *Landsmann,* this means literally a person from the same land. Among Jewish immigrants to this country, it once meant someone from the same town in the Old World; it now often means any fellow Jew. Compare PAESANO.

lapsus linguae   *(LAHP-soohs LIHN-gwai; LAP-soohs LIHN-gway)*
LATIN: slip of the tongue.

The inadvertent but supposedly meaningful "misspeakings" that Freud made infamous in his *Psychopathology of Everyday Life.* His name for *lapsus linguae,* by the way, was the German *Versprechung (fayr-SPREHKH-oohng)*—which also, curiously enough, means "promise."

lasciate ogni speranza, voi ch'entrate   *(lah-shee-AH-teh OHN-yee speh-RAHN-sah voy kehn-TRAH-teh)*   ITALIAN: Abandon hope, all who enter here.

This happy thought greeted the doomed soul at the entrance to Dante's *inferno* (Hell). Since Hell is not quite the kicker it used to be, the expression may profitably be used humorously to announce any place of last (and unlikely) resort: a high school principal's office, for example, or municipal traffic court.

Lebensraum *(LAY-behns-raum)* GERMAN: living space, elbow room.

Non-Germans came to know this word in the most unpleasant of contexts. In the 1930s, as the German chancellor Hitler sent his soldiers into first the Sudetenland, then Austria, and finally Czechoslovakia, he justified his action by an appeal to *Lebensraum:* the German *Volk* were too cramped, they needed breathing room. A remarkably blunt and callous admission of what most imperialists try to disguise: that expansionism is its own reward. See also DRANG NACH OSTEN.

lèse-majesté *(leyz mah-zheh-STAY)* FRENCH: treason.

More precisely, "high" treason, because the party being offended here is *majesté.* The term means basically "It hurts the majesty."

le meilleur des mondes possibles *(luh may-YEUR day MOHND poh-SEE-bluh)* FRENCH: the best of all possible worlds.

In *Candide,* Voltaire ridiculed blind optimism in the character of Dr. Pangloss. His philosophy in a nutshell, frequently intoned by the naive Candide, was *"Tout est pour le mieux dans le meilleur des mondes possibles"* (All is for the best in the best of all possible worlds).

l'état c'est moi *(lay-TAH say MWAH)* FRENCH: I am the state.

Benevolent despotism at its most despotic, if not most benevolent, this is the most famous line attributed to France's ROI SOLEIL, Louis XIV. In spite of its bombastic charm, it is of course a model of regal HUBRIS.

Liebchen *(LEEP-chehn)* GERMAN: sweetheart.

This is a common diminutive expressing affection, usually either for a child or for a lover. It means literally "little love."

lingua franca *(LEEN-gwah FRAHN-kah)* ITALIAN: a common language.

This Italian term describing a "Frankish tongue" referred originally to an Italian-based pidgin language used commercially in the Mediterranean during the Renaissance. Dryden described it as a "compound Language, made up of all Tongues, that passes through the Levant." Today we use the term less precisely, to indicate any widely spoken language, especially one that is important in international dealings, civil or commercial. By this broadened definition, Latin was the *lingua franca* of the ancient Mediterranean, French of Enlightenment Europe, and English of this American century.

locus classicus *(LAW-koohs KLAH-sih-koohs; LOH-koohs KLA-sih-koohs)* LATIN: the classic place.

That is, the place in written literature usually cited as authority for, or earliest instance of, a given idea. "REALPOLITIK may have come to fruition in the works of Machiavelli, but the concept's *locus classicus* was the *Republic* of Plato."

lusus naturae *(LOO-soohs nah-TOO-rai)* LATIN: a freak or "sport" of nature.

Literally *lusus* means "game," and the idea is that Mother Nature is playing games when she creates, for example, albinos or four-leaf clovers.

M

macher *(MAKH-er)* YIDDISH: a big wheel, a mover and shaker.

In Yiddish and in German, this means "maker" or "do-er"; a *macher* is the one who gets things done. Sometimes it's the person with the title on the door, sometimes not. Kings and brokers, in spite of their elevated status, may or may not be true *machers;* kingmakers and power brokers always are. When salesmen ask, "Who has the final approval authority for this deal?" what they are really asking is "Who's the *macher?*"

macho; machismo *(MAH-choh; mah-CHEEZ-moh)*
SPANISH: male.

To be *macho* is simply biology. To be addicted to *machismo,* or "maleness," is something else. It involves an attitude not only of male superiority, but also a fascination with virility that leads one to test one's VQ obsessively in games of violence and sexual conquest. See also HOMBRE.

magnum opus *(MAHG-noohm AW-poohs; MAG-nuhm OH-poohs)*
LATIN: great work.

Not just any great work, but an established master's greatest, most memorable achievement. Michelangelo's Sistine Chapel ceiling, Goethe's *Faust,* Beethoven's Ninth—that sort of thing. The term can also be applied to nonartistic ventures: "After all the talk about the Reagan Revolution has died down, his arms-control work will certainly be remembered as his *magnum opus.*"

mal de mer *(mal duh MEHR)* FRENCH: seasickness.

Literally "evil of the sea." Compare the Latin term *nausea,* as in the expression AD NAUSEAM.

malgré lui *(MAHL-gray LWEE)* FRENCH: in spite of himself.

In Molière's comedy *Le Médecin Malgré Lui (The Doctor in Spite of Himself),* Sganarelle plays the part of a physician against his own better judgment. Compare the expressions *malgré moi (mwah),* "in spite of myself," *malgré elle (ehl),* "in spite of herself," and *malgré tout (too),* "in spite of everything."

mañana *(mahn-YAH-nuh)* SPANISH: tomorrow.

It's a stereotype that Mexicans are addicted to *mañanismo,* or putting things off until tomorrow, but a stereotype with some basis in fact: the expression HORA INGLESA suggests the casualness of an *hora* not *inglesa.* Curiously, *mañana* also means "morning"—that is, the *next* morning, when things will get done. "We didn't do much today," my grandfather used to say at night, "but we'll give 'em hell *mañana.*"

ma non troppo   *(mah nohn TROH-poh)*   ITALIAN: but not too much.

One of the few Italian musical terms that is easily carried beyond the concert hall. *Largo ma non troppo* means "slow but not too slow." "I love aerobics—*ma non troppo*" means "I'd just as soon sit this one out."

manqué   *(māh-KAY)*   FRENCH: failed.

Not "failed" as in "He has failed his final exams." The appropriated sense of this epithet is both softer and, in a roundabout way, more revealing. If you are a mechanic *manqué*, it doesn't mean that you don't know a spanner from a lug nut but that knowing the difference has not *made* a difference: you are, *hélas*, still a Chief Financial Officer. Beaudoin and Mattlin cleverly articulate this term's subtle use: If you are being beaten in a argument, they say, try: "Helen, you're a lawyer *manqué*." Meaning: "You are doing better than me, but you're still *not* a lawyer, you bitch." As this example implies, the expression has the approximate sense of English "frustrated." The idea is amateur excellence, falling just short of the Big Time. Thus, a garden variety café existentialist might be described as a "Sartre *manqué*." Or, in the worst quip I've ever heard, *"Homo sapiens* is a monkey *manqué."*

mare nostrum   *(MAH-reh NAWS-troohm)*   LATIN: the Mediterranean.

This proprietary Roman expression, meaning literally "our sea," is seen sometimes on old maps. Not to be confused with COSA NOSTRA, "our thing."

mariage de convenance   *(mah-ree-AZH duh kohn-veh-NÃHS)* FRENCH: marriage of convenience.

As, for example, one agreed upon to avoid taxes, save on living expenses, or allow one partner entrance into the country. Before the idea of marrying for love came into vogue about a century ago, the *mariage de convenance* was the only kind of marriage there was, and in traditional societies it still is. In most of the world, it must be admitted, marrying for love is inviting inconvenience: romance is only an option for the financially secure.

maven *(MAY-vehn)* YIDDISH: expert.

From the Hebrew for "understanding." Julia Child is a *maven* on French cuisine, Henry Kissinger on international relations. "If you're such a *maven,* why ain't you rich?"

mazel tov *(MAH-zl tawf)* YIDDISH: congratulations.

Mazel in Hebrew means "luck," and *tov* means "good," but as Leo Rosten sagely points out, *Mazel tov* must be used with more care than the ubiquitous English "Good luck." The basic rule is that it's used to signify the completion of a happy event, not its anticipation. You say *Mazel tov* to the law student when she has passed the bar exam, not on the night before she takes it.

mea culpa *(MAY-ah KOOl-pah; MAY-uh KUHL-pah)* LATIN: my fault.

Uttering a *mea culpa,* ideally while beating your breast, is merely a ritualized way of saying "I was wrong, I'm sorry." Roman Catholics, leaving nothing to chance, specify a tripartite admission in the Latin Mass: *"Mea culpa* (beat the breast once), *mea culpa* (beat twice), *mea maxima culpa* (beat a third time)." The *maxima* means "very serious." This kind of thing can be overdone, of course, but it can also be underdone: one wonders what the fate of Richard Nixon's presidency might have been had he yelped a few *mea culpas* over Watergate rather than stonewalling it, pristinely, to destruction. Notice that *culpa* gives us "culpable," "exculpate," and "culprit."

meden agan *(MAY-dehn AH-gehn)* GREEK: nothing in excess.

Few peoples have been as obsessed with the notion of limits as the ancient Greeks. This maxim, inscribed on the Temple of Delphi, counsels the pilgrim to be aware of his own limits—to avoid HUBRIS and to keep to the middle way. Compare ARISTON METRON, AUREA MEDIOCRITAS.

megillah *(meh-GIH-lah)* YIDDISH: a long, boring story.

If Sergeant Joe Friday had been Jewish, he might have said, "Just the facts, ma'am, not the whole *megillah.*" The term occasionally refers to any Big Production (a wedding, a Senate hearing) that is weighted down with details and delay, but the more common meaning is a detailed story, typically one that has been heard many times before. The original of such stories is the Book of Esther, and in fact the Hebrew meaning of *megillah* is the "scroll" (of Esther). Esther is neither a particularly long nor a particularly boring story, however. Leo Rosten explains that the book's bad reputation comes from the fact that it is read aloud, in its entirety and in Hebrew, to Jewish congregations during the holiday of Purim—while they are enduring the final hours of a daylong fast.

memento mori *(meh-MEHN-toh MAW-ree)* LATIN: a reminder of death.

The marking crosses that Mexicans put on accident sites, the ashes that Catholics bear on Ash Wednesday, the Jolly Roger flag of the pirate, the warning *nosce tuam horam* ("know your hour") on medieval clocks— all these are types of *mementote mori*. We are less eager to be reminded of our mortality than, say, the Victorians were, so such mementos have gone out of fashion, except among fringe members of society—punk rockers, bikers—who make a fetish out of the desperateness of the human situation.

ménage à trois *(may-NAHZH ah TRWAH)* FRENCH: a threesome.

Usually, but not necessarily, sexual. Technically this refers to a more or less permanent living arrangement, since *ménage* literally means "household." But in these more frivolous times, even one-night stands with three principals may be referred to, loosely, as *ménages à trois*.

Mene mene tekel u-pharsin *(meh-NAY meh-NAY teh-KAYL oo-fahr-SEEN)* ARAMAIC: Your number is up.

These words, written by a mysterious hand at the feast of the impious King Belshazzar, are interpreted by Daniel to mean that the king's reign is about to end. The prophet's reading, given in Daniel 5:25–28, is as follows: *"Mene:* God has numbered the days of your kingdom and brought it to an end; *tekel:* you have been weighed in the balance and found wanting; *u-pharsin:* and your kingdom has been divided and given to the Medes and Persians." The king is slain that same night. Hence our expression "the handwriting on the wall" to indicate an impending disaster.

mens sana in corpore sano *(mehns SAH-nah ihn KAWR-paw-reh SAH-noh)* LATIN: a healthy mind in a healthy body.

The Roman ideal, expressed in this famous phrase from Juvenal's *Satires,* was of mental and physical soundness united. The extreme distortions of dimwitted jock and flaccid egghead are modern innovations.

mensch *(mehnch)* YIDDISH: human being.

In German, *Mensch* means simply "human being." In Yiddish it takes on the specialized connotation of "nice guy": to be *menschlich* is to be upright, trustworthy, decent; to display *menschlichkayt*—the German equivalent just means "human nature"—is to have nobility of character. It's an odd twist to the term, considering that Jews, probably more than any other Western people, have suffered the barbarities inherent in human nature. Perhaps the explanation lies in the fact that pious Jews seem to share a kind of neo-Aristotelian view of human nature: viciousness and ignorance are seen as unnatural to humans rather than as expressions of the species' darker tendencies.

If *mensch* is sanguine and progressive in this sense, however, it is definitely regressive in another, for it betrays the same androcentric reductionism that makes "man" stand in English for "mankind." Logically *mensch* could be applied, and idiomatically it should be applied, to "nice girls" as well as nice guys; there is no reason one's BUBBELAH could not say, "Joanie, be a *mensch* and make me some tea."

meshugge *(meh-SHUH-guh)* YIDDISH: crazy, strange, nonsensical.

Jews use *meshugge* to mean crazy as the GOYIM use "batty" or "nuts" —with a whiff of good humor and indulgence. It is not a clinical equivalent of "mentally infirm." Similarly, one may speak of a clowning or slightly eccentric friend being a *meshuggener* (if he's male) or a *meshuggene* (if she's female) without in the least implying pathology: silly, unconventional, or stupid behavior of almost any kind may qualify for being called *mishegas* (literally "insanity"). "Did you go to the bargain basement sale last Thursday?" "As much as I need a new hat, I make it a point not to mix with *meshuggenes.*"

métro-boulot-dodo   *(MEH-troh BOO-loh DOH-doh)*   FRENCH: the same old routine.

A recently coined *litanie d'ennui,* which, in Geneviève's apt phrasing, sums up "the drudgery and routine of the Parisian worker's life." Or anybody else's, for that matter. *Métro* here means the subway; *boulot* is street slang for a job; *dodo* is baby talk for sleep. The next time you are confronted with "What's up?" try shelving the "Not much, what's with you" and substituting: "Just the old *métro-boulot-dodo. Et vous?*"

mezza mezza   *(MEH-dsah MEH-dsah)*   ITALIAN: so-so.

An Italian equivalent of the French COMME CI COMME ÇA, this means literally "half and half." Compare ASÍ ASÍ and COSÌ COSÌ.

Milchmädchenrechnung   *(MIHLKH-may-chehn-REHKH-noohng)*   GERMAN: faulty reasoning.

Literally "milkmaid's reckoning," this word may refer to any ill-thought-out scheme or speculation, from poor carpentry to poor government. Keynesians might accuse supply-siders of dabbling in *Milchmädchen-rechnung*—and vice versa.

miles gloriosus   *(MEE-lehs gloh-ree-OH-soohs)*   LATIN: a boastful, "glorious" soldier.

The term comes from the title of Plautus's second-century play, but it has had a long, vaguely ridiculous history. A few highlights: D'Artagnan in *The Three Musketeers,* Shaw's "chocolate soldier" in *Arms and the Man,* and—in our own boastful century—the various incarnations of Rambo. Ollie North comes from the same school, but he has a little too much SAVOIR FAIRE to be a true *gloriosus.*

mirabile dictu   *(mih-RAH-bih-leh DIHK-too)*   LATIN: amazing to say.

A common Roman expression of astonishment. Impressive if used with some restraint, and only in situations where you are truly wide-eyed. Mary Lou Retton's second "10" vault, maybe, or the reappearance of

Gary Hart on the political scene. Not to be confused with *horribile dictu* *(haw-REE-bih-leh),* "horrible to say," which of course should be used even more sparingly.

modus operandi *(MAW-doohs aw-pehr-AHN-dee)* LATIN: way of doing things.

Typically heard in crime shows in its abbreviated form M.O.—meaning the alleged perpetrator's crime signature—this expression may more generally refer to anybody's standard operating procedure, or S.O.P. To paraphrase an old cliché, "There are three M.O.s: the right M.O., the wrong M.O., and the Army M.O. Here we do things the Army M.O."

modus vivendi *(MAW-doohs vee-VEHN-dee)* LATIN: way of living.

A MODUS OPERANDI may be good, bad, or indifferent to the actors; a *modus vivendi* almost always involves a certain degree of difficulty, or more precisely of accommodation. People who are having trouble getting along—business partners or spouses—establish a *modus vivendi* to make the best of a troubled situation. "They've agreed to fight only on Thursday afternoons—and those, let me tell you, are doozies. It's strange, but a *modus vivendi.*"

Moirai *(MOY-rai)* GREEK: the Fates.

Often used substantively as "Fate," *moirai* means basically "the givers of merit," that is, those who mete out your due. In Greek myth there were three Fates: Clotho the spinner (of your life's thread), Lachesis the measurer, and Atropos the cutter. No one could undo what these three had done, but that does not quite justify the use of *moirai* as a synonym for the Arabic KISMET. The Greeks, far less fatalistic than their Oriental cousins, believed in a kind of Hellenic KARMA: one's lot in life was what one deserved and not a result of mere chance.

el momento de la verdad *(ehl moh-MEHN-toh day lah vehr-DAHD)* SPANISH: the moment of truth.

Now used generically to mean any critical moment, it originally referred to that moment in a bullfight where the bullfighter poises for the kill: that instant of fatal suspension just before he plunges in the sword.

momser *(MAHM-zer)* YIDDISH: bastard.

"Bastard" in the specific, genealogical sense and the more general, derogatory one. But *momser,* like GONIF, is a tricky word: it can also be used to express approval, as of someone who is tricky but clever. "Clever little bastard, isn't he?" might be expressed, without a loss of ambiguity, as "What a little *momser* he is." Leo Rosten's caveat is worth repeating: "Don't call anyone a *momser* to his face unless you are on friendly terms; and don't call a child a *momser* unless you are sure Papa or Mama will not be offended."

mordida *(mohr-DEE-dah)* SPANISH: tip, bribe.

The Latin American equivalent of BAKSHEESH, this word means literally "little bite." It is not an optional gratuity. If you expect to enter Mexico, for example, plan on greasing a few palms along the way, for the Mexican definition of customs fees is, shall we say, peculiar. The official agents all expect their little bites, and if you stand on principle, refusing to pay, you will find yourself standing a long time.

morituri te salutamus *(maw-rih-TOO-ree tay sah-loo-TAH-moohs)* LATIN: We who are about to die salute you.

Supposedly the line of greeting that Roman gladiators gave to the emperor and his entourage before entering the arena. Useful, as Ehrlich points out, as an entry line before an examination.

mot juste *(moh ZHUEST)* FRENCH: the right word.

Those who "always know just what to say" have an ample store of *mots justes:* a *mot juste* is the perfectly appropriate word (or phrase) for a given occasion. It may be a BON MOT, but it need not be; a *mot juste* at a funeral would probably not be funny. Useful as a disguise in those moments where something is on the tip of your tongue; it's less clichéd to say "The *mot juste* escapes me"—with an air of cavalier insouciance, of course—than to admit your bewilderment.

le mouton à cinq pattes *(luh moo-TŌH ah sank PAHT)* FRENCH: anything unattainable or impossible.

A charmingly pithy figure of speech, which means literally "the sheep with five feet." Certainly a homier and more accessible image than our convention about chasing rainbows, it is perfect in the mouth of a cynic: "A balanced budget? General disarmament? A good ten-cent cigar? Wonderful ideas, to be sure. Unfortunately, *moutons à cinq pattes.*"

muchacha; muchacho *(moo-CHAH-chuh; moo-CHAH-choh)* SPANISH: girl, boy.

Muchachos is often used familiarly between adult males, especially when reliving their childhoods: "All right, *muchachos,* let's ride!"

mullah *(MUH-lah)* ARABIC: religious leader.

Taking the Iranian *mullahs* as "mere" religious figureheads was a major misconception of American foreign policy in the 1970s. Actually, because of the nature of Muslim fundamentalism, these theocratic bosses are much higher on the political scale than Jewish rabbis or Catholic bishops; perhaps their closest equivalents would be the elders of a Mormon or Calvinist community, or the lamas of old Tibet.

mutatis mutandis *(moo-TAH-tees moo-TAHN-dees)* LATIN: with the necessary adjustments made.

Literally "having changed what had to be changed." "Our legal department is reviewing the contract renewal now, and we'll get you the papers, *mutatis mutandis,* by Friday morning."

Narrenschiff *(NAH-rehn-shihf)* GERMAN: ship of fools.

Das Narrenschiff was a popular social satire written in 1494 by Sebastian Brant. He used the conceit of an ocean journey, as Chaucer had used that of the pilgrimage to Canterbury, to highlight the foibles of his era's social classes. The work reached English-speaking audiences through Alexander Barclay's 1509 translation *Ship of Fools.* Katherine Anne Porter, in 1962, resuscitated the framing device, and the title, to examine the fancies of a new generation of rational imbeciles. The term may aptly be applied not only to our common "ship of life," but narrowly to any organization whose best people are not at the helm. "This company's management is so confused, they ought to rename the place Narrenschiff, Inc."

nascitur *(NAHS-kih-toor)* LATIN: He or she was born.

Frequently found on old gravestones, abbreviated as *nasc.* or simply *n.* "Geo. Wm. Fletcher, nasc. 1791, ob. 1859." See also AETATIS, OBIIT.

née *(nay)* FRENCH: born.

Used to indicate the maiden name of a married woman. "Mrs. Janice Belbottom, *née* Schwartz" means that Mrs. Belbottom was born Janice Schwartz. This word can also be used in its feminine *(née)* and masculine *(né)* forms to indicate a name change for professional purposes: "Judy Garland, *née* Frances Gumm; Cary Grant, *né* Archibald Leach."

nel mezzo del cammin di nostra vita *(nehl MEH-dsoh dehl kah-MEEN dee NOHS-trah VEE-tah)* ITALIAN: in the middle of the road of our life.

The mid-life crisis is not a modern invention. Dante had his over 600 years ago, as he acknowledges in this opening line of his *Divine Comedy.* The rest of the line is *"mi ritrovai per una selva oscura"* (I found myself in a dark wood).

nemesis *(NEH-meh-sihs)* GREEK: retribution.

The active principle of divine retribution, personified as the goddess Nemesis, sometimes as the goddess Dike, or Justice. *Nemesis,* to the ancient Greeks, is what kept everything in its place. It worked like an agent of Hellenic KARMA to give those drunk on HUBRIS their proper due. Today it functions more broadly to mean "undoing," as in "Waterloo was Napoleon's *nemesis"* or, to speak bathetically (see BATHOS), "My *nemesis,* when I diet, is chocolate chips."

Nephelokokkygia *(NEH-feh-loh-koh-kue-GEE-ah)* GREEK: Cloud Cuckoo Land.

This is the name of the city to which the feathered (and featherbrained) characters repair in Aristophanes' *The Birds;* hence it's any realm of abstract or fatuous ideas—a utopia (from Greek *ou topos,* "no place") for airheaded schemers. "There's only one country I know of where a balanced budget might work, and that's Nephelokokkygia."

ne plus ultra *(nay ploohs OOL-trah)* LATIN: the best

Literally "no more beyond," this refers to anything that cannot be improved upon. "As far as the picaresque goes, *Candide* is the *ne plus ultra* of the genre."

n'est-ce pas? *(nehs PAH?)* FRENCH: Isn't that so?

The standard French "agreement tag," equivalent to the English "Right?" and the German "NICHT WAHR?"

nicht wahr? *(nihkht VAHR?)* GERMAN: Isn't that right?

Wahr means "true" and *nicht,* "not," so this extremely common expression functions in German exactly as N'EST-CE PAS? does in French: it solicits agreement by offering the opportunity for disagreement, generally in situations where there would be no reason to disagree. Not recommended in political observations such as "The Republicans really have a SCHWEINHUND platform this time, *nicht wahr?*" Much more appropriate in safe conditions, such as applauding a January thaw: "Lovely weather today, *nicht wahr?*"

nihil obstat *(NIH-hihl AWB-staht)* LATIN: Nothing stands in the way.

That is, in the way of its being printed. This phrase, which appears in many Catholic publications, is the diocesan censor's certification that nothing inside offends faith or morals. Thus it is a kind of grass roots–level rubber stamp of the local bishop's IMPRIMATUR. I once heard the term used maliciously in an old movie whose name I've forgotten. Two thieves, left alone in an unlocked prison cell while the turnkey went for his lunch, debated whether they should honor their word that they would not try to escape while he was absent. *"Nihil obstat,"* one said, and they were gone.

nisei *(NEE-say)* JAPANESE: second generation.

A *nisei* is the son or daughter of Japanese immigrants who is born and raised in the United States: it was this generation that felt the brunt of injustice during the internment of Japanese-Americans in the 1940s. The *nisei* are children of the *isei,* or "first generation," and parents of the *sansei,* or "third generation." This last term should not be confused with the martial arts honorific *sensei,* which means roughly "teacher."

noblesse oblige *(noh-BLEHS oh-BLEEZH)* FRENCH: the responsibilities of rank.

Rank here meaning social rank or what used to be known as "privilege." Webster has this expression dating from the 1830s—the era when the Industrial Revolution, and its attendant great fortunes, was running neck and neck with a nascent nationalism and its attendant sympathy for *le peuple.* (See VOX POPULI.) *Noblesse oblige,* which means "nobility obliges," was perhaps a way of averting the inevitable tension: it suggested that the old orders of birth and privilege were not simply parasites of the working classes but had certain duties of generosity and fair dealing, especially with their social inferiors. Andrew Carnegie in this country gave this notion a mercantile twist by suggesting that great wealth implied the responsibility of "giving back" something to the common horde: hence his library bequests.

nolo contendere *(NOH-loh kawn-TEHN-deh-reh; NOH-loh kahn-TEHN-duh-ray)* LATIN: no contest.

Literally "I do not want to contend." In law this is a defendant's plea that neither admits guilt nor proclaims innocence. A person who has entered a *nolo* plea may be found guilty of the charges but will save the mess of an actual trial—and may contest the charges in another proceeding. A useful TERTIUM QUID for those who fear conviction in any case and who wish to cushion the fall by avoiding negative publicity.

non compos mentis *(nohn KAWM-paws MEHN-tihs)* LATIN: not of sound mind.

Seldom seen in its positive form, *compos mentis* ("possessing a sound mind"), this is the standard legal description for someone who is insane. Solicitor's eccentric defense: "Yes, she took four million pounds from the vaults of the Bank of England. But for the three months this operation lasted, she was *non compos mentis.*" See also MENS SANA IN CORPORE SANO.

nom de plume *(nohm duh PLUEM)* FRENCH: pseudonym.

Literally a "pen name." An older variant is *nom de guerre,* "war name," which hints that the taking of cover identities may have originated among spies rather than poets. Both *nom de guerre* and *nom de théâtre* may be used as equivalents of "stage name."

non sequitur *(nohn SEH-kwih-toor)* LATIN: something that doesn't follow.

In formal logic a *non sequitur* (the Latin simply means "It doesn't follow") is a faulty conclusion arrived at by violating a principle of sound reasoning. A common example is false generalization. In the sentence pair "I saw that Chinese guy hotwire my car" and "All these Chinese are dirty thieves," the second sentence doesn't follow from the first. In everyday usage, a *non sequitur* can be any statement that seems out of place, or off the point, in a conversation. "She has adopted the dart board principle of organization. Her observations are one *non sequitur* after another."

nosce te ipsum *(NAWS-keh tay IHP-soohm)* LATIN. Know yourself.

The Latin equivalent of GNOTHI SEAUTON, this was transmuted in the death-conscious Middle Ages into a frequently cited MEMENTO MORI: *nosce tuam horam (NAWS-keh too-ahm HAW-rahm),* or "Know your hour." That is, be aware of the hour of your death. This was commonly written on clock faces, which must have made telling time a lot of fun.

nosh *(nahsh)* YIDDISH: snack, something to eat.

The German verb *naschen* means to nibble, particularly sweets, on the sly. A *nosh* is thus technically a little bite. But only technically: I once had a three-hour dinner that was referred to ironically as "a pretty good *nosh.*" The word also is used as a verb: "Let's *nosh* before going to the movie." Less frequently you hear *nosher* and *noshing.* The person who picks at the canapés before they are ready to be served is an unregenerate *nosher;* what she is doing is *noshing.*

nouveau riche *(NOO-voh REESH)* FRENCH: a newly rich person; newly rich (n. & adj.).

The best known of three French expressions indicating the arrival of new money. This one, which simply means "new rich," and *parvenu,* which means roughly "one who has come," entered English in the early nineteenth century, when "liberal" ideas and social mobility were transforming European conceptions of class. The third term, ARRIVISTE, or "arriver," came in around 1900, when the industrial fortunes of the Gilded Age were again mixing old and new "barons" socially—much to the chagrin of the old. All three terms have the general sense of "upstart."

nudge *(noohj)* YIDDISH: a pest, nag, or bore.

The similarity to English "nudge" is not accidental, for *nudge* is what Rosten calls "Yinglish." Note the different pronunciation, however—and the fact that a *nudge* is a little less blatant, and generally whinier, than someone who would physically nudge you. It can also be used as a verb: "If you don't stop *nudging* me about fixing the windows, I'm going to jump out of one."

nunc aut nunquam *(noohnk aut NOOHN-kwahm)* LATIN: now or never.

Probably this was the expression in the back of Julius Caesar's mind when he was deciding whether or not to cross the Rubicon. See ALEA JACTA EST.

O

obiit *(AW-bih-iht)* LATIN: he or she died.

It is sometimes assumed that the ancients confronted death more squarely than we do. Maybe, but *obiit* is poor evidence. The Latin verb *obire* means "to go to" or "to go over"—a reference, perhaps, to the River Styx and certainly no less euphemistic than our modern expression "to pass over." *Obiit* is found on many tombstones, abbreviated as *ob.:* "nasc. 1801, ob. 1893." It also gives us "obituary." See AETATIS SUAE and NASCITUR.

obiter dictum *(AW-bih-tehr DIHK-toohm)* LATIN: a passing remark.

Legally, this is a comment made in a judicial opinion that has no immediate bearing on the case at hand, although it may have indirect bearing on future cases. A performer might call it an "aside" or a "one-liner." In general conversation *obiter dicta* are offhand, often digressive remarks that for some reason are memorable. "Oscar Wilde's patter was hopelessly disorganized; the entire charm of his presence lay in the brilliance of his *obiter dicta.*"

odi et amo *(OH-dee eht AH-moh)* LATIN: I hate and I love.

Of Catullus's many lines immortalizing the turmoils of passion, this is probably the best remembered and certainly the most succinct. The bland modern equivalent might be "You can't live with 'em and you can't live without 'em."

olla podrida *(OH-yah POH-dree-dah)* SPANISH: hodgepodge, stew.

Like the French equivalent *potpourri,* this expression means "rotted pot" and probably refers to the ancient custom of disguising spoiled food by serving it in a stew. The literal meaning is forgotten today, and the negative connotation of eclectic messiness is fainter and, usually, nonculinary. "Tax reform was absolutely essential to clean out the *olla podrida* of the old code."

omphakes eisin   *(ohm-FAH-kehs AY-sihn)*   GREEK: sour grapes.

This catchphrase originated in Aesop's fable about the high-hanging grapes and the fox who, being unable to reach them, dogmatically proclaimed them sour. Literally the expression means "They are sour." The fable is so well known that the subject "grapes" is left out, and understood. In Greek, as in English, the phrase is pungently applicable to losses you do not want to acknowledge. "The Wynford account went to our chief competitor, but it really wasn't much of an account"—that's a classic statement of *omphakes eisin.*

orbis terrarum   *(AWR-bihs teh-RAH-roohm)*   LATIN: circle of lands.

An old expression for "the world." The circle *(orbis)* referred to was the ring of countries around the Mediterranean—a name that itself means "in the middle of the lands."

o tempora! o mores!   *(oh TEHM-paw-rah oh MOH-rays)*   LATIN: O the times! O the customs!

Two thousand years ago, Cicero attacked his antagonist Catiline in the Roman Senate by denouncing their common epoch with this expletive: the times and the customs were so dreadful that they permitted the existence of a Catiline. For anyone who feels that things are declining, the comment works just as well today. It also works humorously, in one of the worst puns I've ever heard. Man in an exotic seafood restaurant, exclaiming on the peculiarity of the fare: "Oh, tempura. Oh, morays."

Ôtez le fumier, le coq meurt   *(OH-tay luh foo-mee-AY, luh kohk MEUR)*   FRENCH: Take away the dung, the rooster dies.

Geneviève, who knows her scatology as well as anyone, attributes this stab at French pomposity to Jean Cocteau. The *coq* is the country's national emblem, the *fumier* the gallocentric bullshit (all right, rooster shit) that goes to swell the nation's pride. The quip refers to the poet's fancy that his homeland is *un coq sur un fumier,* or "a rooster on dung." The antichauvinist sentiment is, of course, equally applicable to other nations.

outré *(oo-TRAY)* FRENCH: exaggerated, excessive.

Since *outré* basically means "beyond," the best equivalent might be the 1960s Americanism "far out." "I didn't mind the first time he pierced his ear, but two on each side, that's really *outré.*" *À outrance (ah oo-TRÃHS),* roughly "to the extreme," has the specific meaning of "to the death." Peacetime activities may be *outré;* combat may be carried *à outrance.* Compare DE TROP, RECHERCHÉ.

oy vey *(oy-VAY)* YIDDISH: Woe is me.

"Woe is me" is the technically accurate translation, since *vey* is from German *Weh* ("woe") and since the expression is the truncated form of *Oy vey iz mir.* But—and this is a critical but—*Oy vey* almost never means "Woe is me" in the literal sense. As Leo Rosten says nicely, "*Oy* is not a word; it is a vocabulary," and *Oy vey* is "an all-purpose ejaculation" used to express "anything from trivial delight to abysmal woe." It has the same portmanteau flexibility as the English expressions "Oh boy," "Holy shit," and "Wow." "*Oy,* could I go for a pizza right now." "*Oy,* what a miserable day for a picnic." "He won the lottery? *Oy vey.*" The possibilities are endless.

P

pace tua *(pah-keh TOO-ah)* LATIN: with your permission.

I have heard William F. Buckley, Jr., use a variant of this expression, replacing the *tua* ("your") with the name of the person whose permission he is asking—so that the effect is "with apologies to." I can't recall the exact wording, but it was something like "I tremble for my country, *pace* Jefferson, when I reflect that God is just." The construction seems a bit liberal to me, but a William Buckley can always invoke QUOD LICET JOVI NON LICET BOVI.

paesano *(pai-ZAH-noh)* ITALIAN: friend, buddy.

The literal meaning is "country person," and it is a comment on Italy's peasant heritage that the term is not infrequently applied, with a good deal of shoulder-clapping added in, among lifelong urbanites who simply share the same "old soil." *Paesano* has the same sense in Italian as

LANDSMANN in German and Yiddish; it's less political than the Spanish CAMPESINO.

panem et circenses *(PAH-nehm eht kihr-KEHN-says)* LATIN: bread and circuses.

Juvenal's caustic comment on the dull cupidity of the Roman mob. "Circus" here means the imperial games, including chariot races and gladiatorial combat. The full quotation is *"Duas tantum res anxius optat, panem et circenses"* (They worry about getting only two things: bread and games). The sad lesson to be drawn from this comment—a lesson that numerous demagogues have taken to heart—is that if you feed and entertain the masses, they will be docile to your will.

paparazzi *(pah-puh-RAH-tsee)* ITALIAN: photographers of celebrities.

Ron Gallela and his ilk. Federico Fellini popularized the term in his 1960 film *La Dolce Vita,* where obnoxious Paparazzo represented the breed.

Papierkrieg *(pah-PEER-kreeg)* GERMAN: red tape.

Literally "paper war," and not to be confused with the "paper chase" of competitive academia. When you go up against a government, legal, or business bureaucracy and are immediately engulfed in fawning subordinates, daunting subparagraphs, and multiple submissions, you are engaged in a *Papierkrieg.* Such a war is a tedious kind of *Blitzkrieg,* perpetrated by an unseen, and unseeable, enemy.

par excellence *(pahr ehx-ah-LĀHS)* FRENCH: the best, preeminent.

A useful little fillip that gets its flair from being attached to the end, rather than the front, of a noun. "Jerry is the consummate golfer, the eighteenth-hole wonder *par excellence."* Do not say "She is a *par excellence* driver." The literal meaning is "by excellence," and it should not be confused with *par exemple:* that means simply "for example."

pari passu *(PAH-ree PAH-soo)* LATIN: at an equal rate.

"Josh has never been one to play favorites. He's destroying his marriage and his business *pari passu.*"

parti pris *(PAHR-tee PREE)* FRENCH: prejudice.

Literally "the side taken," presumably without adequete consideration of the other side. "Lincoln didn't care one way or the other about slavery. The only *parti pris* he had was pro-Union."

passe-partout *(PAHS pahr-TOO)* FRENCH: master key.

What it really means is "pass everywhere," which explains the master key usage, and also a more arcane one mentioned by Newmark: a "blanket passport," whatever that might be. If you really want to be RECHERCHÉ about this one, though, you should talk to your local picture framer; in that profession the term means a special mat, matting paper, and method of framing.

passim *(PAH sihm)* LATIN: here and there, scattered.

This editor's or indexer's indication that a topic is covered at various places in a book or article comes from the verb *pandere,* "to stretch or spread out."

pax *(pahx)* LATIN: peace.

We usually see this word today accompanied by a nationalistic adjective. The *pax Romana* was the period of relative rest that ancient Rome enforced on its subject territories. The *pax Britannica* was that which existed under British imperial sway. Journalists who do not count "local unrest" and "wars of national liberation" sometimes refer to this century as that of the *pax Americana.* And *Newsweek* even spoke recently of a *pax Japonica,* indicating Japan's primacy in international markets.

per diem *(pehr DEE-ehm)* LATIN: by the day.

One can work intermittently rather than on a regular schedule or be paid a daily retainer rather than a regular salary: both cases are arrangements *per diem.*

perestroika   *(pehr-ehs-TROY-kah)*   RUSSIAN: restructuring.

One of the two "new ideas" that Mikhail Gorbachev has brought to the Soviet state in the 1980s—the other being the concept of GLASNOST. Gorbachev himself would probably not put quite so fine a point on it, but basically what he means by *perestroika* is the loosening of the traditional Soviet strictures against private property and private enterprise: that is, the introduction of greater incentives for individual economic activity. The devil's definition would be "capitalization."

persona non grata   *(pehr-SOH-nah nohn GRAH-tah)*   LATIN: an unwelcome person.

Like NON COMPOS MENTIS, this term is seldom seen in the positive. The technical meaning of *persona grata* ("pleasing person") is of a diplomat officially acceptable to a foreign country. When such a dignitary becomes *non grata,* it means he (or his country) has offended the host nation. More generally it means anyone uninvited or fallen from social grace. "After I failed to send a note of regret to the marchioness, I was *persona non grata* for two seasons."

un petit cinq-à-sept   *(ãh PEH-tee SÃK-ah-SEHT)*   FRENCH: an afternoon "quickie."

Well, not that quick: the term means "a little five-to-seven," and it refers to an adulterous liaison during the day, en route from the office to the home.

pièce de résistance   *(pee-EHS day ray-zihs-TÃHS)*   FRENCH: showpiece.

Originally a gastronomic term, indicating the show-stopping dish of a banquet, *pièce de résistance* is now used more broadly. "The *pièce de résistance* of their tax package is the dramatic windfall profits clause." *Résistance* perhaps because such a *pièce* is something that no one could resist: it would be a piece overcoming resistance.

pied-à-terre *(pee-ehd-ah-TEHR)* FRENCH: an apartment in town.

Literally "a foot on the ground." This is a second (or third) apartment, which a homeowner can use on those occasions when he or she is away from a primary domicile. "Hotel prices are so dreadful these days, I find it cheaper to maintain a *pied-à-terre* for the three days a month I'm in London."

piropo *(pih-ROH-poh)* SPANISH: a street "compliment."

Piropos are the inescapable comments—ranging from the flowery and polite to the raunchy—that Latin men hurl at attractive women whom they have no intention of getting to know. The conventional response is to ignore the speaker or to giggle, demurely, with one's friends. It is not considered appropriate to deck the jerk.

pis-aller *(pees-ah-LAY)* FRENCH: a last resort.

Literally "to go the worst." "Gorgonzola is my preference. Roquefort if you can't find it. Blue cheese only as a *pis-aller.*"

plus ça change *(ploo-sah-SHĀHZH)* FRENCH: the more things change.

This is the protasis of an aphorism usually attributed to journalist Alphonse Karr (1808–90). The apodosis is *plus c'est la même chose (ploo say lah mehm SHOHZ)*, so that the entire quip might be translated "The more things change, the more it's the same old story." Among cynics at least, the barb is well enough known that you can get the right touch of world weariness with the first three words alone: this is best done with a quick rise-and-fall on the *change*, a roll of the eyes, and a general air of "I told you so."

Karr wrote a satirical periodical entitled *Les Guêpes (The Wasps)* in the politically unstable 1840s and is supposed to have written his one lasting BON MOT in January of 1849—one month after the French people, against Karr's public urging, elected Louis-Napoléon Bonaparte president. Two years later, after the president had declared himself emperor, Karr shrugged his resignation and went to Nice. There—no doubt following Candide's advice—he switched from politics to the more serious business of gardening.

pobrecito *(poh-bray-SEE-toh)* SPANISH: poor little one.

A common expression of affection, sympathy, or both. The feminine form is *pobrecita*. Both are particularly effective if used ironically. "Only a 97 on the math final? *Pobrecito.*"

poco a poco *(POH-koh ah POH-koh)* SPANISH: gently, carefully.

Literally "little by little." "How do you draw an elephant through a keyhole?" *"Poco a poco."*

politikon zoon *(poh-LIH-tee-kohn ZOH-ohn)* GREEK: a social animal.

Aristotle's classic definition, in the *Politics,* for a human being. Thrown off by the cognate, many translators give this as "political animal," a rendition that suggests, too narrowly, the world of ballot boxes and back rooms. *Polis* was the ancient Greek word for "city" or "city state," and what Aristotle meant was that true human beings—as opposed to non-Greeks, or barbarians—were civilized, social, in a word urban. "I couldn't live in a place without subways. I'm a *politikon zoon* through and through."

pons asinorum *(pohns ah-see-NOH-roohm)* LATIN: bridge of asses.

Any difficult or insoluble problem—one that would be as difficult as leading a balky jackass across a bridge. The prototype is supposed to be the Euclidean proposition that the base angles of an isoceles triangle are equal; proving this, or trying to, evidently made asses out of ancient geometry students.

post hoc ergo propter hoc *(pawst hawk ehr-goh PRAWP-tehr hawk)* LATIN: after this therefore because of it.

The logical fallacy that attributes a causal connection to two events which may be merely sequential. Suppose it rains every time I start to wash my car. Concluding that my washing brings on the rain would be an example of *post hoc ergo propter hoc* reasoning.

pravda *(PRAHV-duh)* RUSSIAN: truth.

This is the name of the major party-supervised newspaper in the Soviet Union. The other paper is *Isvestyia,* and the names of these two state organs have given rise to a familiar Russian joke: *V Pravda net izvestii i v Izvestii net pravdy,* or "In *Pravda* there is no news, and in *Isvestyia* there is no truth."

prêt-à-porter *(PREH-tah-pohr-TAY)* FRENCH: ready to wear.

That is, off the rack rather than from a designer's collection. "She may shop *prêt-à-porter,* my dear, but she looks like *haute couture."*

prima facie *(PREE-muh FAH-kee-eh, PRAI-muh FAY-shuh)* LATIN: self-evident, apparent.

Literally this means "at first appearance." The typical usage is legal, and in law a *prima facie* case is one that seems sound at first glance: it may or may not hold up under further examination. The same general sense holds beyond the law. "She was swimming fully clothed in the public fountain, singing fast-food jingles and smelling of wine. I would say, *prima facie,* she was drunk."

primavera *(pree-mah-VEH-rah)* ITALIAN AND SPANISH: spring.

Probably a contraction of *prima verde,* meaning "first green." Botticelli's 1477 allegory *Primavera* is among the most famous of QUATTROCÈNTO paintings.

primus inter pares *(PREE-moohs ihn-tehr PAH-rehs)* LATIN: first among equals.

This logical impossibility is often real enough. Consider the quarterback of a football team, managing a group whose members are equally important to success. Or the Speaker of the House of Representatives, who exercises more authority than his or her fellow representatives but still only has one vote. Ehrlich points out helpfully that, if we are speaking of women in groups, the correct phrase is *prima inter pares.*

prix fixe   *(pree FEEX)*   FRENCH: fixed price.

Referring to a set price menu choice, where everything from appetizer to dessert is included in the single figure. An old-fashioned term for this is *table d'hôte* ("host's table"), as opposed to a menu *à la carte* ("from the card"), where you make individual selections and pay individually for them.

pro bono   *(proh BAW-noh)*   LATIN: for the public good.

Short for *pro bono publico*. This refers to legal work, undertaken at reduced or waived fees, which is thought to in some way further the public interest. A tax attorney who represents an environmentalist group free of charge, for example, is engaging in *pro bono* work; a lawyer who offers free counsel to a friend being sued for divorce may be just as high-minded, but his sacrifice would not count as *pro bono* because it would not be *publico*.

pro forma   *(proh FOHR-mah)*   LATIN: for form's sake.

That is, lacking serious intent or interest. "I detest these royal receptions, but as the Queen is my second cousin, I will make a *pro forma* appearance."

pronto   *(PROHN-toh)*   SPANISH: quickly, right away.

"Sure looks like a twister to me. Let's get into the storm cellar *pronto*." Not to be confused with the Italian *pronto*, which is what you say when you pick up a ringing phone.

pro rata   *(proh RAH-tah; proh RAY-tuh)*   LATIN: prorated.

This is short for *pro rata parte*, "according to a fixed part," that is, in proportion. "Since I missed the final consultation, I'll be submitting a *pro rata* bill."

prosit   *(PROH-ziht)*   LATIN: to your health.

Often erroneously thought to be a German toast, *Prosit!* is actually a Latin expression meaning "May it be beneficial." In case you're interested in the linguistic technicalities, the word is the third person singular, optative mood, of the verb for "to benefit, to do good," *prodesse*.

(The optative, by the way, is the "wishing" mood, from the Latin *optare*, "to wish for.")

pupik *(POO-bihk)* YIDDISH: navel.

Leo Rosten gives numerous uses of Slavic *pupik* in Yiddish expressions; the more colorful include "Thanks in the *pupik*" ("Thanks for nothing") and "I've had it up to my *pupik*" ("I'm fed up"). Part of the inherent humor of the word no doubt derives from its similarity to "pubic," and in fact the commonest usage in my experience humorously conflates the English and Yiddish homonyms. It's the description of *couture* DÉCOLLETAGE as "a dress that's cut clear to her *pupik.*"

qua *(kwah)* LATIN: as.

This one is almost pure pretension, and I include it so you can field it, not use it. "If we consider the candidate *qua* candidate, rather than as a potential governor, we can see that his failings are considerable." The words *"qua"* and "as a" in this sentence perform exactly the same function; you decide if the obscurity is worth it.

quae cum ita sint *(kwai koohm EE-tah SIHNT)* LATIN: therefore.

A stock phrase in classical Latin literature, this means, word by word, "Because these things are so." There's nothing special about it except that it's classical Latin—which lends a certain panache to ordinary transitions: "I failed three courses this term and assaulted the dean. *Quae cum ita sint,* I'm being expelled."

quandoque bonus dormitat Homerus *(kwahn-DOH-kway BAW-noohs DAWR-mih-taht haw-MAY-roohs)* LATIN: Even good Homer nods off sometimes.

This observation from Horace's *Art of Poetry* reminds us that even geniuses have their off moments. It can function as self-exculpation ("This dinner didn't come out quite the way I hoped it would, but *quandoque . . .*"), but because of the riskiness of comparing oneself to Homer, it is safer as an excuse for others' blunders.

Quatsch   *(kvahch)*   GERMAN: nonsense, stupid talk.

This is a kind of Teutonic mixture of CAUSERIE and "balderdash." One might refer to the Edward Lear–Ogden Nash school of poetry as a *Quatschschule,* or dismiss an insipid conversationalist as "a mere *Quatscher.* Compare Yiddish *kvetch,* which quite incidentally also refers to unwanted chatter. One who is both insipid *and* intrusive might be called, one supposes, a *kvetcher-kvatcher.* Like the militantly ignorant art buff about whom a victim once remarked, "His explanation of Jackson Pollock was so convoluted that I could hardly tell the pish from the posh."

quattrocènto   *(KWAH-troh-CHEHN-toh)*   ITALIAN: the   fifteenth century.

Literally "the 400," that is, the 1400s. It refers generally to the art styles of such painters as Donatello and Botticelli, and more generally to anything that happened in their century. The use of this term, as of CINQUECÈNTO, is an example both of how influential Italy was to the nineteenth-century concept of the Renaissance and of how easy it is to be pedantic. *Quattrocènto* is merely a code word: it shows you long ago read your Janson. The best usage I have ever encountered of this term was from a friend who insists, coyly, on consistency. "I will be happy to call Botticelli *quattrocènto,"* he says, "if you will call Fellini *novecènto."*

quel dommage   *(kehl doh-MAHZH)*   FRENCH: what a pity.

As the cognate makes clear, the literal sense here is "what damage"— that is, what an injury has been done. The legalistic tone is softened in idiom, and the expression appears frequently in situations where the "damage" is slight or nonexistent. It carries sarcasm well: "Your stock only rose ten points this quarter? *Quel dommage."*

quelle barbe   *(kehl BAHRB)*   FRENCH: what a bore.

This expression is typically accompanied by a stroking of the cheek with the back of the fingers—which refers to the literal meaning "What a beard." The logic is not fully apparent. Perhaps the deep message is "This person is so long-winded that I will grow a beard before he finishes." In a superb example of Gallic balance, the word *rasoir* (razor) also means bore.

quid pro quo   *(kwihd proh kwoh)*   LATIN: a fair exchange.

Literally "this for that." It's a legal, as well as idiomatic, term indicating the necessity of mutual back-scratching, especially in business and politics. "Yes, I can promise you Greenfield, Congressman; which cabinet seat is my *quid pro quo?*" The *Oxford English Dictionary* says of "quid" as English slang for a pound that it is "of obscure origin." My guess is that is truncates this phrase: a "quid" would have been what a buyer gave in exchange for the "quo" he had purchased.

¿Quién sabe?   *(kee-EHN SAH-bay)*   SPANISH: Who knows?

Often expressed with a visible or understood shrug, as if a question just asked were unanswerable. Pop etymologists give this cliché—especially common in Mexico—as the origin of Kemo Sabe, Tonto's pet name for the Lone Ranger. Remembering that *tonto* in Spanish means "fool," it may be best to utter the phrase with an air of mock obtuseness: "Was Einstein right? *Quién sabe?*"

Quis custodiet custodes?   *(kwihs koohs-TOH-dee-eht koohs-TOH-days)*   LATIN: Who will guard the guardians?

A fundamental question of order in any state, this is posed by Juvenal in his *Satires,* in the relatively trivial context of wondering how to secure loyalty among guards hired to protect wifely virtue. The idea goes back to Plato's *Republic,* where the context is broader and more serious: the question there is how to ensure that those hired to enforce the law are to be held subject to it themselves.

qui vive   *(kee VEEV)*   FRENCH: alert.

This comes from an eighteenth-century sentry's challenge, *"Qui vive?"* (roughly, "Who goes there?"). In English it is not seen by itself but always following the preposition *on:* "We've got a good craft and a good crew, but if we want to weather this storm, we've got to stay on the *qui vive."*

Quod licet Jovi non licet bovi *(kwawd lih-keht YOH-vee nohn lih-keht BOH-vee)* LATIN: What is permitted to Jove is not permitted to the ox.

This expression suggests that different laws should apply depending on one's station in life. It's an outrageous notion in these democratic times —and very much the way of the world. Blake gives the aphorism a memorable twist in his *Proverbs of Hell:* "One law for the lion and the ox is oppression."

quondam *(KWAHN-duhm)* LATIN: former, erstwhile.

Almost as useless as *qua.* The Romans used it to mean "sometime," past, present, or future. Our idiom restricts it to the past: "My *quondam* business partner has flown to Brazil with the last two weeks' receipts."

R

raison d'être *(RAY-zōh DEHT'r)* FRENCH: reason for being.

That is, something's justification or cause. The *raison d'être* of democracy is the serving of the popular will. The *raison d'être* of commercial television (so a cynic might say) is the distribution of commodities. Make a clear distinction between this term and the similar sounding *raison d'état (day-TAH),* which means "reason of state" and should properly be invoked only in cases of national security.

rara avis *(RAH-rah AH-vihs)* LATIN: a rare bird.

Meaning an extraordinary occurrence, an oddity: A Bible-thumping libertine, a teetotaling Frenchman, a Republican who has never mentioned Lincoln—these are *rarae aves.* Ehrlich says the phrase comes from Juvenal, who speaks of the quintessential rare bird as a black swan— black swans being unknown in the ancient world. The Russians speak, similarly, of a *belaya vorona,* a "white crow." And the Greeks speak of "never" as that time when *korakes leukoi genontai*—when crows turn white.

la raza *(lah RAH-sah)* SPANISH: the race.

The Hispanic equivalent of the "Black is beautiful" ideology of the 1960s is an emphasis on the supposed virtues of *la raza*. It's a quite understandable self-defensive posture among a people whose ethnicity has been despised by Anglo culture; for its dangers, see VOLK.

re *(ray)* LATIN: regarding, with regard to.

This is the ablative form of the noun *res*, meaning "thing," which gives us *res publica*, for "republic." It's in the ablative, perhaps, because the sense of *re* is "with respect to the thing." You see it most often in memos (from the Latin *memorandum*, "it must be remembered"), as an alternative to the "Subject" line.

Realpolitik *(RAY-ahl-poh-lih-TEEK)* GERMAN: a politics of realism.

Commonly associated with Otto von Bismarck, the Prussian statesman who forged a united Germany in the 1860s with a policy of *Blut und Eisen* ("blood and iron"), this term suggests a political philosophy, as Nietzsche might have had it, *jenseits von Gut und Böse* ("beyond good and evil"). The proponent of *Realpolitik* does not ask what is right or what is popular, but only what is possible in a given situation for the furtherance of his own, and his state's (or constituency's), vested interests. "Sure, I'd like to vote for the hospital bill. But I'm a believer in *Realpolitik*. Where are we going to get the money?" It is not a philosophy that is popular—at least publicly—with liberals.

réchauffé *(RAY-shoh-FAY)* FRENCH: warmed up.

The literal meaning refers narrowly to food: *haricots réchauffés* are warmed up beans, and a *réchauffé* is any reheated dish. The spicier usage, however, is transculinary. Beyond the kitchen *réchauffé* is stale news, and something that is *réchauffé* is similarly hackneyed. "I don't object to Friedman on principle; it's just that he's Jefferson *réchauffé.*"

recherché *(RUH-shehr-SHAY)* FRENCH: exotic, affected, "precious."

Basically this just means "researched." The evident idea is that, when you research a topic before going public with it, what you find may be too esoteric for anybody else to understand. An oddly anti-intellectual notion, built into this simple word. The usage comes from the Age of Enlightenment, when it might be supposed that the Really Good Ideas would be obvious—that is, accessible to any person of *raison.* Compare OUTRÉ.

reductio ad absurdum *(reh-DOOHK-tee-oh ahd ahb-SOOR-doohm)* LATIN: reduction to absurdity.

Socrates' favorite style of argument. It involves allowing your opponent his or her premise and then showing how it leads, inevitably, to an insupportable conclusion. Of course this is easier to do when, like Plato, you write both sides of a dialogue yourself. It's a little harder to reduce to absurdity someone who is trying to do the same to you.

requiescat in pace *(reh-kwee-EHS-kaht ihn PAH-keh; reh-kwee-EHS-kaht ihn PAH-chay)* LATIN: rest in peace.

By pure linguistic accident, the acronym for this Latin term is the same as that for its English equivalent: *R.I.P.* The mood of the Latin is optative: *"May* he or she rest in peace."

retroussé *(ruh-troo-SAY)* FRENCH: turned-up.

In French you can have a *retroussé* trouser cuff, or shirt end, or even mustache. In English the most common appearance is nasal: what we call a "snub" or "button" nose the French call a *nez retroussé.*

Revenons à nos moutons *(RUH-veh-nōh ah noh moo-TŌH)* FRENCH: Let's get back to the subject.

As a debater's point—cutting and reasonable at the same time—this expression can hardly be equalled: the only other comment I know that imparts quite the same sense of officious one-upmanship is the supercilious "Do I see a concrete referent?" The literal meaning is "Let's return to our sheep," and Beaudoin and Mattlin comment slyly that this makes the expression largely useless "unless you run around with shepherds." Actually, as they well know, it's a perfect way to escape from a corner: as soon as the conversation begins to divagate beyond the limits of your particular expertise, you can blame the entire detour on the other person by implying bluntly that *he* has forgotten the flock. I do not know where the expression started, and I am far too demure to wonder aloud what the first errant shepherd might have been doing when reminded that the subject was sheep.

risorgimento *(rih-sor-jih-MAYN-toh)* ITALIAN: resurgence, revival.

In the early part of the nineteenth century, Italy was a patchwork of tiny duchies and disparate states—a politically disorganized affront to those who recalled the noble past of the Renaissance and, before that, of ancient Rome. The call for a resurgence of bygone glories—in a liberal, unified Italy—was raised in the 1830s by Giuseppe Mazzini and given a standard in 1847 by Count Cavour, when he founded the newspaper *Risorgimento*. That call was answered by, among many others, the flamboyant Giuseppe Garibaldi, and by 1870 Italy was one country.

ritorno d'immagine *(rih-TOHR-noh dih-MAH-jee-nay)* ITALIAN: a public relations boost.

According to Sergio Perosa, writing in *The New York Times* on Italian literary awards, both public and private sponsors are fond of these awards because, for a few million lire, they earn the sponsoring organization much "positive feedback"—the same logic that keeps our corporate warchests pumping life into public television. The phrase, Perosa says, is television jargon; the literal meaning is "return of image."

roi fainéant *(rwah FAY-nay-āh)* FRENCH: a figurehead or factotum.

Literally, this means a "do-nothing king," but it may profitably be applied to any ineffectual leader. According to Democratic legend, our last reigning *roi fainéant* was President Eisenhower. ("Have you heard about the Ike doll? You wind it up and it sits for four years.") Peter Drucker uses the term pointedly in an essay on the corporate "bored" of directors: "Years of experience indicate that the board has become a *roi fainéant*, an impotent ceremonial and legal fiction."

roi soleil *(rwah soh-LAY)* FRENCH: the Sun King.

The most popular epithet applied to France's Louis XIV, who for over half a century was as close to an absolute ruler as has been seen in the modern world. His reign, which managed to involve France in wars with virtually all of Europe, was undeniably brilliant on the home front. Among those who profited from his patronage were Molière, Jean-Baptiste Lully, Jules Mansart, and a countless host of sycophants at Versailles. It was Louis whose glittering life-style both emblemized and defined the notion of *gloire;* it was because he gave France her hour in the sun that the epithet, fittingly, survives. See also ANCIEN RÉGIME; L'ÉTAT C'EST MOI.

roman à clef *(roh-MÃH nah KLAY)* FRENCH: a "key" novel.

A novel in which real persons are given fictional names, so that there is a secret, unexpressed meaning or key *(clef)* to the story. Not the same as a historical novel or as a straight biography, this genre achieves its popularity by teasing rather than telling.

roseau pensant *(roh-ZOH pãh-ZÃH)* FRENCH: a thinking reed.

Pascal, in his *Pensées,* acknowledged the fragility of human life but supposed it was ameliorated by reason. *"L'homme n'est qu'un roseau, le plus faible de la nature, mais c'est un roseau pensant"* ("Man is only a reed, the weakest in nature, but he is a thinking reed").

ruse de guerre *(ROOZ duh GEHR)* FRENCH: a ruse of war.

Such as, for example, the use of a white flag to set up an ambush (not unknown in the annals of warfare) or (to cite an example SUI GENERIS) the use of the so-called Trojan horse by the Achaean horde at the gates of Ilium. See TIMEO DANAOS ET DONA FERENTES.

S

salaam *(sah-LAHM)* ARABIC: peace.

The full form of the traditional Islamic greeting is *Salaam alaykem,* or "Peace be with you." This is usually shortened to *salaam.* A *salaam* is also the gesture of respect which may accompany the greeting: a low

bow done with the right palm placed on the forehead. Compare the
Hebrew greeting SHALOM.

samizdat *(SAH-meez-daht)* RUSSIAN: self-publishing.

In any place with rigid central censorship, the distribution of written
materials tends to fall out of the state-approved tracks and to function
clandestinely. In the Soviet Union, this type of SUB ROSA distribution
is called *samizdat.* The *samizdat* network consists of isolated typists—
the monkish copyists of their day—and strictly word-of-mouth advertis
ing. There are of course no royalties in this system, but then writers
who must resort to *samizdat* tend not to be rivals to Judith Krantz.

sanctum sanctorum *(SAHNK-toohm sahnk-TOH-roohm)* LATIN:
holy of holies.

That is, the holiest of all places—least accessible to outsiders, most
revered by the privileged. It's fundamentally a religious term, used to
describe, for example, the Christian or Jewish tabernacle. But by extension it can also refer to anything secluded. *Finnegans Wake* might be
considered the *sanctum sanctorum* of Joyceans, and Carlsbad Caverns
a similar "shrine" to the fancier of stalactites.

sang-froid *(sahng-FRWAH)* FRENCH: composure, equanimity.

Idiomatically, sang-froid is imperturbability, or poise in the face of ad-
verse circumstances. It might better be translated, however, by the
American slang term "cool," for its literal meaning is "cold blood." The
dangers of literalism may be observed in unidiomatic, though exact,
translations: "In her response to these attacks, the ambassador displayed admirable cold blood."

sangre azul *(sahn-gray ah-ZOOL)* SPANISH: blue blood.

Rogers says that this expression came out of Moorish Spain, where it
was a Castilian boast of pure-bloodedness. The blue blood of the Moors
was not visible through their dark skin; hence, only Castilians were of
sangre azul.

sans-culotte *(sāh-KOO-laht)* FRENCH: a radical revolutionary.

The original *sans-culottes* (literally "those without breeches") comprised the most radical wing of the uprising during the French Revolution. Today the term may profitably, if not honorably, be applied to anyone left of the speaker. It all depends on where you stand, of course. As the history of the Old and New Lefts has shown, one person's *sans-culotte* may easily be another's fascist lackey.

satori *(sah-TOH-ree)* JAPANESE: enlightenment.

The goal of Zen and, indeed, of all Buddhist discipline. In conventional terms, this might translate as something like "an instant recognition of the meaning—or sublime meaninglessness—of life."

sauve qui peut *(sohv kee PEU)* FRENCH: everybody for himself.

A nonchivalrous, last-ditch CRI DE COEUR, such as one might hear on a sinking ship. The literal translation is "Save himself who can."

savoir faire *(SAH-vwahr FAYR)* FRENCH: social tact.

Literally "knowing how to do." Usually applied to social situations involving the BEAU MONDE. But one can have social graces, of course, at any level of society: the Duchess of Kent would not necessarily display *savoir faire* at a pig roast given on New Guinea—any more than the pig roasters would know "how to do" in the Duchess's own social sphere. See also BIENSÉANCE.

Schadenfreude *(SHAH-dehn-FROY-duh)* GERMAN: malicious glee, gloating.

Strictly construed, this means "hurtful joy." It suggests the sentiment that suffuses even the best of us when we observe a rival, conscious or unconscious, experience a setback. Watching our next-door neighbor's lawn turn brown, hearing about the boss's market losses, seeing the challenger just miss beating one's record—all these involve the not entirely honorable emotion known as *Schadenfreude.*

Schmecht? *(shmehkht)* GERMAN: Do you like it?

Schmecken means "to taste" or "to taste good," and this question usually refers to food. Not always, however. In front of an "action" painting a number of years ago, I overheard this laconic but spirited exchange between one appreciative and one outraged patron: *"Schmecht?" "Schmach." "Shmuck."* (*Shmuck* means "penis" or "jerk"; *schmach* means "disgrace.")

Schnapsidee *(SHNAHPS-ee-day)* GERMAN: crazy idea,

Crazy not as in clinically pathological but as in "stupid." The derivation is obvious: *Schnaps* is hard liquor, *idee* is "idea." "Max has invented everything from bicycle windshield wipers to fire extinguishers for exploding cigars. He doesn't drink. I don't know where he gets his *Schnapsidees.*"

schön *(shoen)* GERMAN: nice, good, beautiful.

The connotation is always good but is seldom limited to the narrow meaning of "beautiful." Often it functions as a mere conversational filler, like English "well" or "OK." "Meet me for lunch tomorrow?" *"Schön,* I'll see you at noon." Dignified into a noun, however—the German is *Schönheit (SHOEN-hait)*—it always has the basic sense of "beauty."

Schweinhund *(SHVAIN-hoohnt)* GERMAN: a low-down character, a dirty dog.

This common stage epithet—simultaneously pejorative, vulgar, and humorous—means simply "pig dog." It illustrates the principle of synergistic insult. To call someone a *Schwein* is bad enough. To add *Hund* is that much worse. But to combine the two generates a certain unsavory TERTIUM QUID the kind of multiplier effect you get in English with an expression like "sneaky bastard."

semper fidelis *(SEHM-per fih-DEH-lihs)* LATIN: always faithful.

Often abbreviated, especially on bumper stickers, as "Semper Fi," this is the well-known motto of the U.S. Marine Corps: what the Corps is faithful *to* is honor, country, and of course itself. Compare *semper paratus (pah-RAH-toohs)*, "always prepared," which is the motto of the

Coast Guard and a kind of Latinate version of the Boy Scout motto "Be prepared"; and the hymn *Adeste fidelis (ah-DEHS-tay),* "Come all ye faithful."

shabbes *(SHAH-behs)* YIDDISH: the Sabbath.

From the Hebrew *shabbat,* meaning "the end of labor." In the Jewish faith this day of rest—on which no work may be performed—lasts from sundown Friday to sundown Saturday.

shalom *(shah-LOHM)* HEBREW: peace.

Jews use this word not only to mean "peace," but also as the typical salutation and farewell: it can thus function as both "Hello" and "Good-bye." One of the direst ironies of Middle Eastern history is that Muslim Arabs use exactly the same word, although they pronounce it *sah-LAHM.* The full greeting, in both tongues, adds to *shah-LOHM/sah-LAHM* the word *ah-LAY-khehm.*

shaygets *(SHAY-gehts)* YIDDISH: a non-Jewish male.

Or, more broadly, a nonreligious Jew. According to Leo Rosten, the term also encompasses a puzzling contradiction: positively it suggests cleverness and charm; negatively, lack of intellectual ambition. Go figure. See also GOY, SHIKSA.

shiksa *(SHIHK-suh)* YIDDISH: a non-Jewish female.

Like SHAYGETS, the term may be broadened to refer to nonreligious Jewish women as well as Gentiles. See also GOY.

shlep *(shlehp)* YIDDISH: to carry, to travel.

From the German *schleppen,* "to drag." The commonest usage refers to lugging things—packages, luggage, or children, for example: "I *shlepped* the kids all over town today." But it's also used to describe unencumbered traveling, when you consider the trip long or unnecessary. "I've taken a little PIED À TERRE just because I don't like to *shlep.* " Used as a noun, *shlep* can mean the trip itself—"Four flights up? What a *shlep*"—or the person doing the *shlepping;* the person is also known as a *shlepper.*

shlock *(shlahk)* YIDDISH: junk.

Not as coarse as DRECK or as demeaning as CHAZERAI, *shlock* means simply cheap, low-quality merchandise. A *shlock-house* is a place that sells used or defective goods; a *shlockmeister* is the agent who arranges the delivery of gifts to television giveaway shows; *shlock rock* is "co-opted" rock 'n' roll, that is, Elvis Presley as done by Muzak.

shmalz; schmaltz *(shmawlts)* YIDDISH AND GERMAN: sentimentality.

Shmalz is outrageous sentiment, generally in works of art, literature, or music. The literal meaning is "fat," and it is hard to divine the connection to sentiment, unless it's that a tearjerker makes us "melt" *(schmelzen)* with emotion. A maudlin production can be *shmalzy,* or *shmalzed up,* or just out and out *shmalz.*

In the movies, incurable diseases always rate high on the *shmalz* index, as witness *Dark Victory* and *Love Story.* But plain sticky sweetness will also do, as for example in *The Sound of Music.* And it's pretty hard to beat unrequited love: *Brief Encounter* and *Casablanca* are two of the *shmalz* classics of all time. They don't hardly make fat like that no more.

shmatta *(SHMAH-tuh)* YIDDISH: cloth, rag.

From the Polish *szmata* for "rag," this means, by extension, anything worthless: a cheap house or car, a trashy novel—any of these might be loosely called a *shmatta.* The term even attaches to people if they are of a sufficiently dishraglike nature: "That apple-polishing *shmatta,* Chairman of the Board? Don't make me laugh!" But the commonest reference is still to clothing. A society matron may dismiss her last season's designer gown as "just a *shmatta";* New York's garment district is *Shmatta* Central.

shmeer *(shmeer)* YIDDISH: a spread; a bribe.

The German *schmieren* means to "grease," and you can grease a palm as well as a wheel. The Yiddish retains this ambiguity, using *shmeer* as a synonym for "grease money" and also to describe anything that can be "smeared"—from paint to a canapé spread. In New York, a "bagel with a *shmeer*" is one that has been spread with cream cheese.

l'shanah tovah *(leh shah-NAH toh-VAH)* HEBREW: Happy New Year.

The standard greeting among Jews at the season of Rosh Hashonah, or New Year. It is a shortened form of *l'shanah tovah tikoseyvu,* meaning "May you be written down for a good year" in the Book of Good Deeds that decides your fate.

shtick *(shtihk)* YIDDISH: stage business; a characteristic gimmick.

Derived from German *Stück,* for "piece," this originally meant "bit" in the simplest sense: "Let me have another *shtick* candy, please." Now it usually means "bit" in the theatrical sense: the peculiarity of a given performer, such as Johnny Carson's pencil tapping or Jack Benny's celebrated deadpan. By extension it can also mean one's business in general: "What's your *shtick,* Harry?" "I'm in plastics."

shtup *(shtoohp)* YIDDISH: push; fuck.

From the German *stupsen,* "to push." It's more frequently heard in its obscene sense than as a synonym for "push" or "shove." In this sense it functions, like English "fuck," as both noun and verb: one may *shtup,* and also have (or be) a *shtup.* This word has been less fully assimilated into American slang than, for example, SHMUCK or PUTZ, and unless you know your company extremely well, you are advised to avoid it. Rhyme the vowel with *u* as in "push," not as in "fuck" or "boot." If you're going to be vulgar, do it right.

sic *(sihk)* LATIN: thus.

Meaning "It is thus in the original." *Sic* is an editor's aside, in the middle of a quoted passage, indicating that the spelling (or, rarely, the logic) of a preceding word or phrase, while doubtful, stands this way in the original text. "As the lesser Marxian is reputed to have said, 'Diacritical [*sic*] materialism is a hoax.' " The *sic* here says to the reader: I know the proper term is "dialectical," but the author I'm quoting doesn't.

sic semper tyrannis *(sihk SEHM-per tih-RAH-nihs)* LATIN: thus always to tyrants.

John Wilkes Booth's alleged cry of triumph after he assassinated President Lincoln. Booth was not alone, of course, in thinking Lincoln—and the Union that he stood for—representative of tyranny, although it does seem unfortunate to have such a laudable sentiment attached forever to a deplorable act.

Sic transit gloria mundi *(sihk TRAN-ziht GLOH-ree-ah MOOHN dee)* LATIN: Thus passes away the glory of the world.

This is the fifteenth-century cleric Thomas a Kempis assessing the transitory nature of earthly life. A mighty thought, perhaps too easily travestied, because of the natural response, "Who was Gloria Monday, anyway?"

si Dios quiere *(see DEE-ohs kee-EH reh)* SPANISH: if God wants it.

A common Mexican nod-to-the-most-high, thought appropriate in any situation, from the profound to the trivial, where the assumption of success might bring down retribution: "We can go fishing this afternoon. *Si Dios quiere.*" It's a classic example of the Mediterranean insistence that, whatever you may think you're going to do, the ultimate decision is out of your hands. Compare the Latin DEO VOLENTE, DEO FAVENTE; and the Greek concept of NEMESIS.

Sieg Heil! *(zeeg HAIL)* GERMAN: Victory!

Familiar from World War II films, this was the German *Volk*'s salute to Hitler at many of the Third Reich's rallies. *Sieg* means "victory" and *heil* is "hail"—with the general sense of "Hurrah!"

simpatico *(sihm-PAH-tee-koh)* ITALIAN AND SPANISH: nice, congenial, affable.

A common plaudit in both languages, with the same sense of imprecision as "nice," it may be applied to both things and people. Hackneyed in the Romance tongues, it's still rare enough in English to carry a certain air of chic: "Joe is *molto simpatico*" doesn't have quite the same deadness as "Joe is a nice guy." In Italian, the opposite is *antipatico,* "antipathetic." If Joe's *not* such a nice guy.

sine qua non *(SEE-nay kwah NOHN)* LATIN: anything essential.

Short for *conditio sine qua non,* "a condition without which nothing," and used to describe anything that is critical to the success of an enterprise. "Of the many factors that need to be resolved to bring peace to the Middle East, settlement of the Palestinian question is the one *sine qua non.*"

soi-disant *(swah dee-ZÃH)* FRENCH: so-called, self-styled.

As a Gallic synonym for "so-called," this has little to recommend it: a guiding principle of foreign *nom-*dropping is that the alien phrase should add something to the original—and that is not the case with *soi-disant* as "so-called." As "self-styled," however, the term is richer: it makes the harsher point that the exaggerated reputation has been one of the reputee's own devising. To call Elvis Presley a *soi-disant* guitarist is niggling after a phantom, since he never made that claim for himself. To call Salvador Dali a *soi-disant* genius—that is precisely to the point.

son et lumière *(sohn ay loo-mee-EHR)* FRENCH: sound and light.

As in sound-and-light shows, which since the acid-blasted 1960s have been an integral part of many rock 'n' roll concerts. It should not be assumed that the rock version of the form was the earliest. Brewer, referring probably to the court presentations of the seventeenth- and eighteenth-century Bourbon kings, called them "dramatic spectacles presented after dark and, most advantageously, in an appropriate natural or historic setting." Something like Madison Square Garden.

sotto voce *(soh-toh VOH-chay)* ITALIAN: quietly.

This looks like it means "in a soft voice," but the actual meaning is "in an under voice"—or, roughly, under one's breath. It's one of the few Italian musical terms that have broken out of the concert hall into the street. "That is the ugliest hat I've ever—" "I entirely agree, but *sotto voce* . . . he'll hear you."

Sturm und Drang *(SHTOORM oohnt DRAHNG)* GERMAN: storm and stress.

A late eighteenth-century literary movement of which the most enduring example is Goethe's *Die Leiden des jungen Werthers*. It emphasized energy over reason, the unusual (the medieval, the demonic) over the conventional, the primitive over the "civilized." The expression is more generally used today to suggest these qualities, rather than the movement itself. The 1960s in America saw a resurgence of *Sturm und Drang* sentiment, and it is not incidental that young people expressed it more than most: the sentiment is the very spirit of adolescence.

subito *(SOO-bee-toh)* ITALIAN: quickly, right away.

Uttered as a gentle command, to offset the effects of *domanismo*. It comes from the Latin verb *subire*, which means "to go under" and sometimes "to come after"; something that happens *subito* in Latin comes immediately after something else.

sub rosa *(soohb RAW-sah; suhb ROH-zuh)* LATIN: in secret, in confidence.

Literally "under the rose." Roses have fascinated poets for centuries: they are as much a symbol of mystery and "unfolding" potential in the West as the lotus is in the East. Why should this flower be associated, as the idiom suggests, with secrecy? Perhaps because its multilayered petals make it difficult to get at its true center. Or perhaps, as Ehrlich indicates, because of an old Roman myth in which Cupid, to protect the reputation of Venus (a hopeless task), gives a rose to the god of silence so he will not tell of her affairs. It's as useful an idiom as it is pretty. Indeed, in a world where so much politics is conducted in nervous, guilty whispers, *sub rosa* is the norm, not the exception.

sui generis *(SOO-ee GEH-neh-rihs; SOO-ee JEH-ner-ihs)* LATIN: one of a kind.

Literally "of its own kind," and thus equivalent to English "unique." Like "unique," it admits of no comparative: one can no more speak of a record collection as being "more or less *sui generis*" than one can have a "very unique" butler: either Parker is singular or he is not.

T

tabula rasa *(TAH-boo-lah   RAH-sah;   TA-byoo-luh   RAH-suh)*
LATIN: an empty slate.

In Rome this meant a writing tablet from which the scratched characters (see GRAFFITI) had been scraped clean. John Locke is often associated with the image because, in his *Essay Concerning Human Understanding* (1690), he rejected the popular notion of innate ideas and pictured the newborn human's mind as devoid of impressions—as, in his phrase, "white paper." This notion of the mind as pure potential had enormous consequences for pedagogy, not to mention democracy, and the metaphor *tabula rasa* has entered the idiom to suggest any open-ended or open-minded state. "As revolutionaries we cannot build on the past; we must begin from a *tabula rasa.*"

ta Kaisaros Kaisari *(tah KAI-sah-rohs KAI-sah-ree)*   GREEK: Give the government its due.

In Matthew 22:21 we find Jesus' somewhat quibbling judgment on the ancient dilemma of church versus state: Render unto Caesar the things which are Caesar's, and unto God the things which are God's. The New Testament Greek is as follows: *Apodote ta Kaisaros Kaisari, ta ton theon to theos.* Hardly a solution to the dilemma, but a useful comment nonetheless, especially at tax time. "Should a free citizen be obliged to pay taxes? *Ta tou theou toi theoi,* I suppose."

tant mieux; tant pis *(tãh mee-UE; tãh PEE)*   FRENCH: so much the better; so much the worse.

Tant mieux is an acknowledgment that the situation is even more satisfying than you had hoped for. Particularly appropriate as a retort. Scrooge, warned by social workers that his refusal to aid the poor might lead to their deaths, replied, "Let them die, then, and decrease the surplus population." The same effect might have been achieved more economically with *"Tant mieux." Tant pis* is simply the reverse.

TASS *(tahs)* RUSSIAN: Telegraph Agency of the Soviet Union.

This is the Soviet equivalent of the Western wire services such as UPI and Reuters. In Russian the acronymic title is spelled TACC but pronounced as above.

le téléphone arabe *(luh TEH-luh-fohn ah-RAHB)* FRENCH: word of mouth.

Geneviève has this expression, which literally means "Arab telephone," referring to the spreading of rumors. Perhaps it also refers obliquely to the spreading of anti-imperialist information during the Algerian war for independence. As a Gallic slap at Arab primitivism, it might also register the occupying army's befuddlement at a communications network that could not be tapped.

tempus fugit *(TEHM-poohs FOO-giht; TEHM-puhs FYOO-jiht)* LATIN. time flies.

Or, literally, "Time is fleeing." Vergil was the first to use this now common personification. His conceit makes a nice companion piece to CARPE DIEM.

terra firma *(TEH-rah FIHR-mah)* LATIN: solid land.

The hope of any sailor, especially in the days when sea voyages lasted for months, was to set foot on *terra firma* before he died. In the days of triremes and galleys, no doubt sailors shouted *"Terra firma!"* as enthusiastically as their descendants cried "Land ho!" An interesting sidelight, according to my Cassell's: *terra* comes from *torrere,* "to dry up"—so that the root meaning of "land" is "that which is dry." Just as in the Genesis version.

terra incognita *(TEH-rah ihn-kawg-NEE-tah)* LATIN: uncharted land, the unknown.

No matter how *firma* it might be, ancient *terra* could still be unexplored, and this phrase recalls that reality. Today we use it to mean anything unfamiliar or untried: "I did pretty well up through trigonometry, but calculus was *terra incognita.*" In other words, "Here be dragons."

Compare our appropriation of *incognito* to mean "hidden" or "unknown."

tertium quid *(TEHR-tee-oohm KWIHD; TEHR-shee-uhm KWIHD)* LATIN: a third something.

Used both to indicate an indeterminate component that does not fit into either category of a dichotomy, and to suggest a compromise category (or position) that resolves the dichotomy. In the first sense we might say that the viruses, being neither animal nor plant, represent a zoological *tertium quid*. In the second sense, adopting a Marxist perspective for a moment, we could say that Renaissance capitalists were the *tertium quid* that resolved (or rather complicated) the medieval dichotomy between landowners and serfs.

tête-à-tête *(TEHT-ah-TEHT)* FRENCH: an intimate conversation.

Not necessarily *very* intimate. Just intimate enough to require the two parties to face each other "head to head." Also used as an adjective. "We had a nice little *tête-à-tête* chat" or "We had a nice little *tête-à-tête.*"

Timeo danaos et dona ferentes *(TIH-may-oh DAH-nah-ohs et DOH-nah feh-REHN-tays)* LATIN: I fear Greeks even when they bring gifts.

This is from Book II of the *Aeneid*. The speaker is the Trojan priest Laocoön, who is warning his countrymen not to accept the wooden horse that the Greek army has presented to them, evidently as a peace offering. He's right, of course: the misnamed "Trojan" horse proves the city's undoing, since it turns out to be filled with Greek warriors. Laocoön doesn't fare too well himself. Having offended Athena by attempting to expose the Greek RUSE DE GUERRE, he is choked to death, with his two sons, by two sea serpents. The incident is the subject of one of the most famous of classical sculptures, the marble masterpiece now in the Vatican.

Torschlusspanik *(TOHR-shloohs-PAH-nihk)* GERMAN: last-minute panic.

Literally "door-shutting panic," this refers to any situation where the game might be lost forever if quick chance or action do not intervene.

The authors of *Beyond the Dictionary in German* suggest that it describes the "fear and increased efforts of women in their late twenties or early thirties to find a husband," but it might easily be applied to other cases where the approaching deadline is clearly defined. If there were an American holiday honoring *Torschlusspanik,* it would be December 24 or April 14.

tous pour un, un pour tous *(too poor ĀH, āh poor TOOS)* FRENCH: all for one, one for all.

The unofficial motto of the four heroes in Alexandre Dumas's *Three Musketeers.* In that context it sounds grandly chivalric, but in fact it is in essence the necessary code of any cadre exposed to constant danger. The military services today, whether consciously or not, create bonding by appeal to this sentiment, and as Hunter Thompson showed in his study of the Hell's Angels years ago, it is precisely the code of outlaw bikers.

tout de suite *(toot SWEET)* FRENCH: immediately.

Actually this means "all of the following." The sense seems to be that, when you want something done right away, you are asking for what follows, with some urgency.

tovarich *(toh-VAH-rish)* RUSSIAN: comrade.

Often used in conjunction with a person's title, much like the Germans use *Herr:* "Comrade Sergeant" or "Comrade Professor." The "comrade" sense is strictly post-Revolution. Before 1917 *tovarich* meant "friend," and in nontitular usage it still does.

traduttori, traditori *(trah-doo-TOH-ree, trah-dee-TOH-ree)* ITALIAN: Translators are traitors.

A technical pun suggesting the difficulty of carrying idioms across a language barrier. Interestingly, the same sense of difficulty is contained in the English cognate *traduce,* coming from the Latin *traducere*: it means "to lead across" and "to betray." The common sense here is the old Mediterranean idea that crossing borders—with or without papers —is always risky business. See, for example, MEDEN AGAN.

tranche de vie *(TRÃHSH duh VEE)* FRENCH: slice of life.

As is displayed, for example, in the realistic novels of Zola or the realistic-seeming stories of O. Henry.

trompe-l'oeil *(trohmp LOY)* FRENCH: illusionistic painting style.

The most recent example of *trompe-l'oeil* ("fool the eye") painting is the photorealism of the 1970s and 1980s, but in fact the gimmick goes back a long way. Renaissance artists were fond of mural decoration that promised objects that were not there, depths that were shallower than they seemed. The advent of photography in the nineteenth century did away for a time with the game, and it is hardly surprising that, when *trompe-l'oeil* was reborn a decade ago, artists challenged not plain reality, but the photograph.

le trou normand *(luh troo nohr-MÃH)* FRENCH: the Norman hole.

I don't know whether Normans are greater eaters than the rest of the French or whether they are merely more inventive, but their chief contribution to table matters is a device to help the glutton keep shoveling it in, long after his KISHKES say "Enough." The Romans made room for more food by sticking their fingers down their throats, in a room aptly called the *vomitorium.* The Norman solution is less messy. The *trou normand* is a drink of *calvados*—that heady brandy-type elixir made from the local Calvados apple—and it is supposed to burn a "hole" in your stomach so that, even after twenty or thirty courses, you can get back to stuffing your face. Normans—and now the rest of the country, too—serve the liquor about halfway through a meal. From experience I can say it does the job. And it does it with remarkable flavor: the divine *calva* is not to be confused with the syrups that Americans call apple brandy.

tsuris *(TSOOR-ihs)* YIDDISH: trouble, aggravation.

Taken from the Hebrew *tsarah* for "trouble," this term may refer to difficulties of any degree, from dandruff to bankruptcy. The chief source of parental *tsuris* is children, and vice versa. The United States and the Soviet Union have created entire foreign policies (speaking loosely) out of the desire to make *tsuris* for each other. Remember the Catskill pundit's paraphrase of the Biblical adage: "Sufficient unto the day is the *tsuris* thereof."

tuches *(TOOHKH-ehs)* YIDDISH: buttocks.

The Yiddish and now American connotation of "buttocks" derives from the more general meaning of Hebrew *tahat,* "bottom" or "under." Leo Rosten calls *tuches,* paradoxically, both "common" and "taboo." It is not taboo among my Jewish friends, who use it with the same casual abandon, and with the same connotations, as non-Jews use "ass" or "butt." Of course, as with all gluteamaximal terminology, there is a possibility of sexual, and therefore potentially taboo, implications. The common diminutive of *tuches* is *tush* (rhymes with "push"), and the leering observation "Nice tush" means the same thing as "Nice ass." But sexist innuendo need not be present. A spanking in Yiddish is a *potch in tuches,* or "slap on the behind," and I once heard a decidedly heterosexual friend comment, after a night at the ballet, "Rudolf Nureyev has the greatest *tush* in the world."

U

Übermensch *(UE-ber-mehnch)* GERMAN: overman, superman.

This is Nietzsche's term for the superior being who continually, painfully, regenerates himself by going "over" *(über)* and beyond his own limitations: he (or she) is Nietzsche's answer to Goethe's Faust. In one of the more unfortunate misreadings in cultural history, however, the term was appropriated by German racists in this century and applied to the man *(Mensch)* who was superior to others by virtue of having been born German. This dimwitted skewing of Nietzsche's meaning led ultimately to the Nazis' "super race" fallacy, to Teutonic xenophobia, and to the Holocaust.

ubi sunt *(OO-bee SOOHNT)* LATIN: an elegy.

Ubi sunt in Latin means "Where are . . . ?" An *ubi sunt,* therefore, in earlier times was a piece of writing, usually poetic, that wondered aloud about the passing of greatness—the idea being to alert the listener to the ephemeral nature of his own existence. Shelley's "Ozymandias" is probably the most famous example of the genre in English; François Villon's *"Où sont les neiges d'antan?"* might take first honors in French. In both of these Death is a key player. In our modern versions, sanitized and celebritized, we ask not ruefully but with perky curiosity, "I wonder what Beaver Cleaver's doing now?"

un caso di forza maggiore *(oon CAH-zoh dee FOHR-tsah mah-jee-OH-reh)* ITALIAN: something beyond one's control.

Glendening notes that this expression is employed, somewhat excessively, as an excuse for failings which "quite easily could have been avoided." It functions, then, with the same exculpatory sense as the Spanish impersonal construction: a Mexican would say, "The glass broke itself to me" rather than "I broke the glass"; an Italian might say, "The glass broke—*un caso de forza maggiore.*" The literal meaning of course is "a case of greater force"—the force being the same as that in the French FORCE MAJEURE.

d'un certain âge *(dāh sehr-TĀ nahzh)* FRENCH: middle-aged.

One of the more economical of euphemisms. The literal meaning is "of a certain age."

und so weiter *(oohnt zoh VAI-ter)* GERMAN: and so forth.

The German equivalent of *et cetera,* this means literally "and further in the same way." Abbreviated as *u.s.w.*

Der Untergang des Abendlandes *(dehr OOHN-ter-gahng dehs AH-behnt-LAHN-dehs)* GERMAN: the decline of the West.

The title of German philosopher Oswald Spengler's pessimistic tract on European cultural decay, published just after World War I and popular as a call to arms among the Nazis. Spengler's fatalistic theory of history, in which decline occurred predictably in all civilizations, was largely ignored by his supporters, who supposed the inevitable could be resisted by force of "will." A similar rejection of Spenglerian fatalism is evident among contemporary America-firsters, who trace the Western democracies' current troubles to a collective failure of nerve.

uomo universale *(oo-OH-moh oo-nee-vehr-SAH-leh)* ITALIAN: universal man.

The Renaissance ideal: a courtier equally well versed in the arts of the pen and the lute and the sword—the kind of accomplished *dilettante* ("one who delights") that gives us the catchphrase "Renaissance man." During the CINQUECÉNTO, the paragon was perhaps Leonardo. Today the closest approximation might be a rock star who paints on the side. And they say there's no such thing as Progress.

ur- *(oor)* GERMAN: original.

One of the most useful prefixes in German and, for that matter, in any language. It has an air of primeval mist about it and may be used in any number of on-the-spot agglutinations to instantly age a noun. *Urgermanisch*, for example, is the original, preliterate form of the German tongues. *Ureltern* are older than mere elders: they are one's original, prehistoric ancestors. An *Urbild* is the earliest *Bild* ("picture") of a series, that is, a model or archetype. And an *Ursache* is the first *Sache* ("thing"): in other words, something's cause.

The nice thing about the *ur-* prefix (indeed, about German prefixes in general) is that you can tack it onto any word you wish—German, English, or Ukrainian—and add an accessible fillip to your meaning. A first kiss might be called an *Urkuss*, humanity's first snack the *Urnosh*, the hour of the Big Bang the *Ur-Uhr*.

ut multa paucis verba *(ooht MOOL-lah PAU-kihs VEHR-bah)* LATIN: to make a long story short.

James Rogers gives the origin of this expression as one Pacuvius, a second-century Roman author. The full sentence is *"Ut multa paucis verba obnuntiem"* ("So that I may announce many words in a few").

V

vade mecum *(vah-day MAY-koohm)* LATIN: a constant companion.

Not companion as in chum, but as in something you carry in your pocket. Usually a *vade mecum* (the Latin means "go with me") is a small book, frequently consulted, but it might also be any other small object that accompanies the owner everywhere: the plastic nerd pack of the student grind, for example, or Kojak's ubiquitous lollipop. "Hey, baby, how'd ya like to be my *vade mecum?*" "Sorry, I don't date outside my species."

vae victis *(vai VIHK-tihs)* LATIN: Woe to the vanquished.

Attributed originally to one Brennus, a Gallic chieftain who surrendered to the Romans, in 390 B.C., uttering this mournful sentiment. Given the Romans' traditional treatment of prisoners, he had good reason to be down.

Valhalla *(vahl-HAH-luh)* OLD NORSE: hall of the slain.

The gigantic palace in Norse mythology where dead heroes are received by the god Odin. Their life there reflects their earthly interests. Each day they leave the palace to do battle; their wounds heal by the evening; and they return for firelight feasting in the great hall, where VALKYRIES serve them boar's meat and mead.

Valkyrie *(val-KEE-ree)* OLD NORSE: "chooser of the slain."

In Norse mythology, the Valkyries were attendants of the war god Odin, entrusted with carrying the bodies of slain warriors from the battlefield into VALHALLA. Because of their depiction in Wagnerian opera by often hefty sopranos, "Valkyrie" has come to have approximately the same connotation as the Greek-inspired "Amazon"; it refers to any large or "masculine" (that is, aggressive) woman. In Valhalla, the Valkyrie were cupbearers to the honored dead; they did not, it seems, perform the sexual services of the similar Arabian HOURI.

vamos; vámonos *(VAH-mohs; VAH-moh-nos)* SPANISH: let's go.

Vamos is the origin of the cowboy expression "to vamoose." *Vamos* and *vámonos* are used interchangeably. "I've had enough of this party. *Vámonos.*"

Vaya con Dios *(VAH-yah kohn DEE-ohs)* SPANISH: Go with God.

In other words, goodbye. In these secular times, this is a little less popular a farewell than it used to be—but then so is "God be with ye," which is the origin of our "Goodbye." Les Paul and Mary Ford had a hit song with this title back in the halcyon 1950s.

Veni, vidi, vici *(WAY-nee, WEE-dee, WEE-kee; VAY-nee, VEE-dee, VEE-chee)* LATIN: I came, I saw, I conquered.

This economic expression is attributed to Julius Caesar. Either he sent the witticism as a dispatch to the Senate after he had conquered the Pontus, or he displayed it as a banner in the triumph (parade) that followed the Pontic victory. Its principal value today is in ushering in pontifical debates about "classical" versus "church" pronunciation. Since everyone has heard the line quoted, you are pretty sure of fomenting amusing trouble by proclaiming, when you hear the church *V*s, "We always learned it was 'Way nee, Wee-dee, Wee-kee.' " Or vice versa *(WEE-kay WEHRS-uh).*

verboten *(fehr-BOH-tehn)* GERMAN: prohibited, forbidden.

Thanks to a plethora of wartime movies, this word evokes an entire world of stiff-necked, iron-jawed rigidity: in Nazi Germany, it seems, everything was forbidden. Today the term—which is the past participle of the quite ordinary verb *verbieten*—is widely used in benign circumstances: *Rauchen verboten,* for example, means simply, "No smoking."

¿Verdad? *(vehr-DAHD)* SPANISH: Really?

Literally "Truth?" Italian uses a similar expression, *È vero?* meaning "True?" These terms don't necessarily indicate skepticism, any more than the French and German equivalents N'EST-CE PAS? and NICHT WAHR?

via dolorosa *(vee-ah doh-loh-ROH-sah)* LATIN: the sorrowful way.

Specifically the path that Jesus took to Calvary. Generally any course of action attended by painful consequences. "When I got back from Vietnam I thought my troubles were over; but my *via dolorosa* had just begun."

via media *(vee-ah MAY-dee-ah)* LATIN: the middle way.

That is, the way of moderation. Compare ARISTON METRON, AUREA MEDIOCRITAS, and MEDEN AGAN.

Vive la différence! *(VEE-vuh lah dih-fehr-ÃHS)* FRENCH: Long live the difference.

The difference, of course, is that between the sexes. An old French cliché.

Volk *(fohlk)* GERMAN: people.

Thanks largely to the eighteenth-century writer Johann Herder, modern Germans have had an almost mystical affection for the concept of *Volk*, or what we would call "the folk." The relatively benign aspects of that affection have been the collecting of back-country *Volkslieder (LEE-der)*, or folk songs (Herder was the first to do so) and the positing, in the Romantic era, of a distinctive *Volksgeist (gaist)*, or popular spirit, for each nationality. The demonic side of the *völkische* bent came, of course, under the Third Reich, when *das Volk* was transformed into *das Herren-volk (HEHR-ehn-fohlk)* or "master race." Note also that the Volkswagen bug was Hitlerian Germany's answer to the common person's desire for personal transport: the name means, literally, "people's car."

volte-face *(VOHLT-fahs)* FRENCH: a reversal.

The sense is close to our "about face." "Last year, Senator, you voted for the MX missile; now you're voting against it. Why this sudden *volte-face?*"

vox clamantis in deserto *(vawx klah-MAHN-tihs ihn deh-ZEHR-toh)* LATIN: a voice crying in the wilderness.

The Latin version of a familiar Biblical image: that of John the Baptist in the wastes of Judea, "preparing the way" of the Lord. It appears in the New Testament in the gospel of Matthew, but Matthew is recollecting the Old Testament prophet Isaiah, who seems to predict John's coming in his Chapter 40. This is the chapter, incidentally, from which Handel took the most stirring lyrics for his chorale *Messiah.*

vox populi, vox dei *(vawx PAW-pyoo-lee, vawx DAY-ee)* LATIN: The voice of the people is the voice of God.

This archly democratic message, so modern in its implications, was first articulated around the year 800, by the English scholar Alcuin. He wrote it in a letter to Charlemagne, who can hardly be accused of democratic sympathies. One of those many instances in human history of a good idea whose time had not yet come.

Wanderjahre *(VAHN-der-YAH-ruh)* GERMAN: year of wandering.

A traditional year of travel undertaken by German students as a break from university studies. Intended as a broadening experience, the *Wanderjahre* also served as a last fling of fancy before maturity; hence the connotation of irresponsibility and "time off." Cousins to the custom were the proper English person's Grand Tour and the American's "European experience," the latter of which only fell out of favor in the war-torn 1960s, when leaving school meant the forfeiture of student deferment. What killed the American *Wanderjahre* was the draft.

Wanderlust *(VAHN-der-loohst)* GERMAN: wanderlust.

Wander is the same in English and German, but the German *Lust* means "pleasure" or "delight." So *Wanderlust* is the delight taken in travel. In English the term always applies to someone who is *about* to start traveling, not one who is IN MEDIAS RES. This is because the English idiom takes *Lust* in its English cognate meaning: as a desire for something as yet unobtained.

Weltanschauung *(VEHLT-ahn-SHAU-oohng)* GERMAN: philosophy.

This word is bandied about a great deal in academic circles because it sounds more impressive than it is. "Do you subscribe to the basic tenets of the Sartrean *Weltanschauung?*" may sound like a tough question to field, but there's nothing very mysterious about it. *Welt* means "world" and *anschauen* means "to look at," so this dollar-fifty word simply means "outlook," or the way that you happen to see the world—in other words, your philosophy.

Weltschmerz *(VELT-shmayrts)* GERMAN: world pain, worldweariness.

"World pain" is the literal translation. The sense is of a sentimental grimness, brought on by the sorry state of the world. Part anomie, part ANGST, and part boredom, *Weltschmerz* is an appropriate state of mind, perhaps, only for someone in a crisis: an adolescent or midlife passage, for example. By definition the uneasiness is nonspecific: if you can pin down its cause, it's not *world-*weariness. If you're fifty dollars short on the rent, for example, what you have is not *Weltschmerz* but *Geltschmerz.*

wunderbar *(VOOHN-der-bahr)* GERMAN: wonderful, great.

The Germans are much given to expressions of wonder. The language contains at least four differently suffixed adjectives approximating "wonderful." *Wunderlich* is a little eccentric, being closer in meaning to "queer" or "strange." But *wunderbar, wundersam,* and *wundervoll* are all essentially equivalent. The last of course is the cognate, but the former is more common (in German) as well as being more euphonious. Appropriate as generic praise: for special occasions, go with AUSGEZEICHNET.

Wunderkind *(VOOHN-der-kihnt)* GERMAN: child prodigy.

Literally "wonder child." Like ENFANT TERRIBLE in its most limited sense, *Wunderkind* suggests a youthful marvel, generally one accomplished beyond his years in some intellectual or artistic pursuit. The chief example in European history was the young Mozart. It can also be used, less rigorously, to applaud the achievements of a quite ordinary child—especially one's own. "My Alex is a real *Wunderkind.* Only ten, and he can read the Dow-Jones."

Z

Zeitgeist *(ZAIT-gaist)* GERMAN: spirit of the times.

Since it's been in vogue among social scientists for about a century, this word is most often applied to matters cultural or intellectual: one speaks of the neoclassical *Zeitgeist* of Renaissance Florence, the decadent *Zeitgeist* of Weimar Germany. Just as useful in more mundane areas, however: "Terrorism is no longer an aberration; it has moved into the mainstream of the *Zeitgeist.*"

zolotaya seredina   *(zoh-loh-TAI-yah seh-reh-DEE-nah)*   RUSSIAN: the golden middle.

Or, more commonly, the golden mean. The Russian equivalent of Latin AUREA MEDIOCRITAS and Greek ARISTON METRON, this might prove an invaluable guideline in arms negotiations—assuming basic intelligence on the part of both sides. For that assumption, see KOGDA RAK SVISNET.

Special Categories

Roman Beginnings

The Romans had various terms for "from the beginning." Although they are approximately equivalent in basic meaning, an appreciation of their literal nuances might be helpful if you are about to drag them out in company. All are formed with the preposition *ab (ahb)*, meaning "from."

ab aeterno	ai TEIIR-noh	from eternity
ab incunabulis	ihn-koo-NAH-boo-lees	from swaddling clothes
ab initio	ih-NIH-tee-oh	from the beginning
ab origine	aw-RIH-gih-neh	from the origin
ab ovo	OH-voh	from the egg
ab urbe condita	OOR-beh KAWN-dih-tah	from the founding of the city

The last of this sestet needs explaining. Ancient Romans were (if this is conceivable) even more chauvinistic about their city than modern New Yorkers or Parisians. To them, history itself began with Rome, and they dated all events from its founding. Tradition set this in what we would call 753 B.C., so that our year 53 B.C., for example, would in Rome have been 700 *ab urbe condita*—or, to be more precise, DCCAUC. The abbreviation AUC also stood for *anno urbis condita,* or "in the year of the city's founding." See also AB OVO USQUE AD MALA.

Classical Phobias

Because *phobos* in Greek means "fear," psychologists speak of inordinately strong or irrational fears as phobias (FOH-bee-ahs), and they identify them with predictably arcane Greek (or monstrously Greek-and-Latin) labels. Herewith the technical terms for some common, and some not-so-common, anxiety reactions.

Fear of	Technical term	Pronunciation
bridges	*gephyrophobia*	geh-FIH-roh-
cats	*ailurophobia*	ay-LOO-roh-
closed spaces	*claustrophobia*	KLAWS-troh-
the dark	*erebophobia*	eh-REH-boh-
death	*thanatophobia*	thah-NAH-toh-
dirt, germs	*miasmaphobia*	mee-AZ-mah-
dogs	*cynophobia*	SIH-noh-
fire	*pyrophobia*	PAI-roh-
flying	*aeroplanouphobia*	ah-EH-ro-PLAH-noo-
heights	*acrophobia*	A-kroh-
human beings	*anthropophobia*	AN-throh-poh-
lightning	*keraunophobia*	keh-RAW-noh-
marriage	*gamophobia*	GA-moh-
men	*androphobia*	AN-droh-
mirrors	*kathreptophobia*	kath-REHP-toh-
mice	*myophobia*	MAI-oh-
open spaces	*agoraphobia*	a-GOH-rah-
sex	*erotophobia*	eh-RAH-to-
sharks	*karkharophobia*	kahr-KAHR-oh-
sleep	*hypnophobia*	HIHP-noh-
snakes	*ophidophobia*	oh-FIH-doh-
spiders	*arachnophobia*	a-RAK-noh-
strangers	*xenophobia*	ZEE-noh-

Fear of	Technical term	Pronunciation
thirteen	*treiskaidekaphobia*	trehs-kai-DEH-kah-
water	*hydrophobia*	HAI-droh-
women	*gynecophobia*	GAI-neh-koh-

And one that might have figured in American political history, but didn't. Remember FDR's ringing call to economic recovery, "The only thing we have to fear is fear itself." The supposed condition he was describing, the fear of fear, the Greeks would have called *phohophobia.*

A Sanskrit Sampler

Ever since the Maharishi Mahesh Yogi convinced the Beatles that TM was a hipper acronym than LSD, the West has been deluged with Eastern gurus—some quite earnest, some as phony as a baby-kissing campaigner—who claim to have the key to peace of mind. With their devotees becoming more numerous and more visible, the technical terminology of the bliss-mongers is gradually creeping into our vocabulary. Much of it is, like Western philosophical jargon, almost impossibly abstruse. But the more common terms are accessible:

ahimsa
ah-HIHM-sah

The principle of harmlessness or nonviolence. Gandhi's touted ideal.

ananda
ah-NAHN-dah

Bliss, joy. Also the name of one of the Buddha's favorite disciples, and therefore a popular "new name" taken by today's disciples.

asana
ah-SAH-nah

A yogic sitting posture whose goal, according to Mircea Eliade, is to give the body "a stable rigidity, at the same time reducing physical effort to a minimum."

ashram
ASH-rahm

A community of disciples—that is, their physical home or retreat.

atman
AHT-mahn

Literally "breath" or "soul," *atman* refers both to the quintessential inner self and to the ultimate universal Self which pervades and animates everything.

bhakti
BAHK-tee

Worship, mystical devotion.

bodhi
BOH-dee

Enlightenment, supreme knowledge.

bodhisattva
BOH-dee-SAHT-vah

An enlightened being who, for the sake of all other "sentient beings," refrains from entering *nirvana* until they too are enlightened.

brahman
BRAH-mahn

The universal Soul or divine spirit, and not to be confused with *brahmin,* which is merely a member of the priestly caste. The identity of *atman* and *brahman* is reflected in the old equation *tat tvam asi,* meaning "You are that" or "You are the universe."

chakra
CHAHK-rah

One of the six energy centers ranged from the base of the spine to the brain. Usually depicted as lotuses *(padma),* they represent the path through which the *kundalini* power rises from gross impulse to pure consciousness.

dharma
DAHR-mah

Law (cosmic) or duty (personal). If you are in sync with the universe, of course, the cosmic and personal are one.

guru
GOO-roo

A spiritual guide. Literally the term means "heavy." Thus "My guru is a heavy dude" would be superfluous praise.

kali yuga
KAH-lee YOO-gah

The present era of vice and general imbalance, the "evil age." It is thought to have begun about 5000 years ago; there is no consensus on when it will end.

karma
KAHR-mah

Action and the result of action. One's fate is thought to be largely determined by the *karma* built up in previous lifetimes: thus, if you behave badly in one life, you will pay for it a succeeding one. Often oversimplified as "fate."

kundalini koohn-dah-LEE-nee	Psychic energy, represented as a coiled serpent lying at the base of the spine. One visual metaphor for Enlightenment is the uncoiling of this serpent up into the highest of the *chakras*.
mandala mahn-DAH-lah	A magical design, typically circular and quadranted, used both as a representation of the universe and as an aid to meditation. The word means "circle."
mantra MAHN-trah	A sacred, and secret, sound which a meditator repeats either orally or silently to generate vibrations that enhance inner calm. The word means "murmuring." Many devotees refuse to reveal their *mantras*, while others (like *om*) are public and common formulas.
maya MAI-yah	Illusion; specifically, the illusion that the physical world is real—the fundamental human error.
moksha MOHK-shah	Deliverance from the "karmic wheel," or the cycle of death and rebirth. Also known as *mukti*.
mudra MOO-drah	Literally "seal," a *mudra* is any of countless hand and finger gestures used symbolically in meditation and prayer. The American "OK sign" is curiously identical to one of the commoner *mudras*.
nirvana nihr-VAH-nah	Typically misrepresented as the Eastern "heaven," *nirvana* is actually an ideal state of mind—or rather, to borrow a Zen notion, of no-mind. The word means "extinction," and the person who has attained *nirvana* has extinguished all traces of (painful) desire for the phenomenal world: beyond wanting, he is therefore beyond loss.

om
ohm

The original and ultimate *mantra, om* has been called "the seed-syllable of the universe." There is nothing private or arcane about this sound: it is thought to be of value to all beings. *Om* is probably being murmured, right this second, by millions of people around the globe.

prana
PRAH-nah

Breath: usually used in a more physical sense than *atman. Pranayama* are breathing exercises used in meditation.

samadhi
sah-MAH-dee

The highest stage of concentration, in which subject and object become one: the word means roughly "integration." This is the true goal of meditation.

samsara
sahm-SAH-rah

The tedious round of death and rebirth, created by *karma,* from which the seeker desires to escape. The centrality of evanescence in the Indian world view is suggested by its literal meaning: "passing through."

shantih
SHAHN-tee

Peace. The word is best known in the West, perhaps, as a prayer coda in T. S. Eliot's *Wasteland.*

siddhi
SIH-dee

An occult or magical power supposedly achieved by certain *yogis* as a result of meditation. Among the most commonly announced *siddhis* are levitation, teleportation, and invisibility.

sutra
SOO-trah

Literally "thread" or "string" (of precepts), a *sutra* is an aphoristic teaching. Not to be confused with *sudra,* which is the name of the lowest Indian caste.

yoga
YOH-gah

Literally "yoking," the term refers both to the philosophy engendering union of the individual with the divine, and to the various practices accompanying it: these may be as simple as *hatha* ("forceful") yoga bodily exercises, and as refined as *raja* ("kingly") yoga exercises aimed at mastery of the mind.

yogi
YOH-gee

One who practices yoga; the female practitioner is a *yogini*.

French Ballet
Terminology

The seeds of ballet were sown in Italy, in the lavish court spectacles of the CINQUECENTO. But the form first truly flowered in neighboring France, particularly at the court of Louis XIV. Not only did the monarch dance himself—it was his 1653 appearance as the sun in a court ballet that earned him the nickname LE ROI SOLEIL—but he also established the West's first national dance academy, the enormously influential Académie Royale de Danse. Its dancing masters created the technical vocabulary that ballet dancers still employ today. So that you will not commit the unpardonable sin of confusing a *pirouette* with a *jeté*, I give the most common terms here.

arabesque ah-rah-BEHSK	The dancer stands on one leg with the other leg extended behind and one or both arms stretched out in front. Literally "Arabian."
assemblé ah-sāhm-BLAY	The dancer jumps up, bringing the feet together ("assembling" them) in the air before landing.
attitude ah-tee-TUED	The dancer assumes a pose, or "attitude," standing on one leg, raising the other (with the knee bent) either behind or in front, and holding one arm up, the other to the side. This position was popularized by the nineteenth-century dancer Carlo Blasis, who copied it from Renaissance sculptor Giovanni Bologna's statue of Mercury.
barre bahr	The supporting rail, or "bar," used in stretching and other leg exercises. The term also refers to the exercise segment of a ballet class.

battement
baht-MÃH

A "beating" movement, of which there are numerous variations: the common element is that the dancer raises one leg up and away from the other. *Battements* constitute a principal feature of *barre* exercises.

bourrée
boo-RAY

Originally a seventeenth-century dance from the Auvergne region, a *bourrée* is a series of small, rapid steps which suggest that the dancer is gliding across the ground.

cabriole
kah-bree-OHL

Literally "caper." The dancer leaps up, beating the two straight legs together, as far off the vertical as possible.

changement
shãhzh-MÃH

Literally a "change" of the feet. The dancer jumps up from a set foot position, reversing the position before landing.

chassé
shah-SAY

The dancer slides one foot out to the front, back, or side and then follows, or "chases," it with the other.

entrechat
ãh-truh-SHAH

The dancer leaps vertically, rapidly crossing and uncrossing the feet before landing. Each such movement counts as two: thus an *entrechat six* means three flutters of the feet. The world record *entrechat douze* (six full flutters) is held by Wayne Sleep of the Royal Ballet.

fouetté
foo-eh-TAY

Literally "whipped." The dancer spins on one leg, whipping the other leg around in a rapid *rond de jambe en l'air* and creating a spinning top effect. The most famous use of the technique is in Act 3 of *Swan Lake*, where Odile performs thirty-two successive *fouettés*.

glissade glee-SAHD	Literally a "sliding" step, allowing the dancer to move from one position to another on the stage without either foot leaving the floor.
jeté zheh-TAY	Literally "thrown," a *jeté* is any leap from one foot to the other. The soaring leaps that dancers do with the legs extended as if in a split are called *grands jetés,* or "big jumps." It sounds so much less pedestrian in French.
pas de deux pah duh DUE	A "step of two," and not to be confused with the two-step. *Pas* here is used in the sense of "dance" or "performance," so that a *pas de deux* is merely a dance of two people: typically, they are the prima ballerina and her partner. The term can also apply to larger units, however: a set piece for five dancers would be a *pas de cinq,* one for fourteen a *pas de quatorze,* and so on.
pirouette pih-roo-EHT	The dancer does a 360-degree turn on one leg. The other leg may be extended or placed in an *arabesque* or *attitude* position. However, in the simplest and most common *pirouette,* the free foot is drawn in toward the supporting knee, giving the familiar spinning top effect.
plié plee-AY	A "bending" of the knees performed with both feet flat on the ground or with a very slight raising of the heels. *Pliés* cushion the shock of landings, impart spring to jumps, and help to loosen the leg muscles: because of this last effect, every ballet class begins with *plié* practice.

pointe
pwãht

The "point" or tip of the toes. Female dancers and, very rarely, male dancers perform *sur les pointes,* or "on point" in special shoes. Interestingly, these were created only at the beginning of the nineteenth century, when ballet was already two hundred years old. Before then the dancer's greatest elevation was achieved by standing on the balls of the feet, with the toes spread for balance: this technique is still known as *demi-pointe,* or "half point."

port de bras
pohr duh BRAH

"Carriage of the arms." It refers specifically ʽto the proper positioning of the hands and arms and, more generally, to upper body carriage. Torso exercises at the *barre* are thus referred to as *port de bras.*

relevé
ruh-leh-VAY

The "raising" motion that is performed when a dancer goes to *pointe* or *demi-pointe.*

rond de jambe
rõh duh ZHAHMB

Literally "circle of the leg." The dancer stands on one leg and describes a circle with the other. The circle may be made on the floor (giving a *rond de jambe à terre*) or in the air *(en l'air).*

sauté
soh-TAY

Any leap or jump. We speak of frying as sautéeing because of the "dancing" action of hot oil.

sissone
see-SOHN

The dancer leaps from two feet onto one foot, performing a scissorlike opening and closing of the legs while in the air.

tour en l'air TOOR āh LAYR	The dancer jumps straight up and performs a circular turn (literally a "turn in the air") before landing. Most male dancers are able to negotiate two full twists (a *double tour*), and a very few can do triples. In the Soviet ballet, incidentally, *tour* is another term for *pirouette*.
variation vah-ree-ah-see-ŌH	Balletomanes do not speak of a *pas d'un;* the proper term for "solo dance" is *variation*.

For related musical terms, see Italian Musical Terms.

Italian Musical Terms

"It's gotten so that if I don't hear that *appogiatura* in the *basso ostinato,* I feel that something's been left out." Boy, me too. This question came straight off the airways, from a local classical music interview show. So that you may avoid feeling the same pangs of *imbecillità musicale* that I felt when I heard it, here is a smattering of musician's jargon from the language that has dominated it since the Renaissance. First, the most common *tempo* ("time") marks, given in order of increasing speed.

largo	LAHR-goh	large, broad
lento	LEHN-toh	slow, sluggish
adagio	ah-DAHZH-ee-oh	slow
andante	ahn-DAHN-tay	walking
moderato	moh-deh-RAH-toh	moderate
allegretto	ah-leh-GREH-toh	"a little allegro"
allegro	ah-LEH-groh	cheerful, brisk
presto	PREHS-toh	quick, fast

Note also three varying tempos:

accelerando	ah-cheh-leh-RAHN-doh	accelerating, speeding up
ritardando	rih-tahr-DAHN-doh	"retarding," slowing down
rubato	roo-BAH-toh	"robbed"; the performer may play freely, "robbing" the value of one note from another

Next, a selection of directions indicating the appropriate mood or expression of a piece:

appassionato	ah-pah-see-oh-NAH-toh	passionately, intensely
con brio	kohn BREE-oh	brightly, with spirit
dolce	DOHL-chay	sweetly
furioso	foo-ree-OH-zoh	wildly, madly
giocoso	joh-KOH-zoh	humorously
grandioso	grahn dee-OH-zoh	with dignity
grazioso	grahts-ee-OH-zoh	gracefully
lacrimoso	lah-kree-MOH-zoh	tearfully, sadly
lamentoso	lah-mehn-TOH-zoh	mournfully
maestoso	mai-STOH-zoh	with "majesty," dignity
vivace	vee-VAH-chay	in a lively manner

Third, the most common dynamic markings, indicating the degree of softness or loudness:

pianissimo	pee-ah-NEE-see-moh	very soft
piano	pee-AH-noh	soft
mezzo piano	MEHD-zoh pee-AH-noh	"middle soft"
mezzo forte	MEHD-zoh FAWR-tay	"middle loud"
forte	FAWR-tay	loud
fortissimo	fawr-TEE-see moh	very loud
crescendo	kreh-SHEHN-doh	increasing in loudness
decrescendo or *diminuendo*	day-kreh-SHEHN-doh dee-mee-noo-EHN-doh	decreasing in loudness

The range of male voices is typically given in English: bass, baritone, and tenor. Female ranges are in Italian, though. Here they are, from the lowest to the highest:

alto or	AHL-toh	high
contralto	kohn-TRAHL-toh	"counter-high"
mezzo soprano	MEHD-zoh soh-PRAH-noh	"middle soprano"
soprano	soh-PRAH-noh	superior, above
coloratura	koh-loh-rah-TOO-rah	"colored" soprano

A *coloratura* is one capable of performing trills and *arpeggios* with ease. *Coloratura* is also used to describe a musical passage that contains such difficult exercises.

The following are common performance directions, indicating to the player how he or she is to attack a particular passage:

glissando	glee-SAHN-doh	"gliding" up and down in a rapid, fluid fashion
legato	leh-GAH-toh	smoothly, with no break between notes
obbligato	oh-blee-GAH-toh	"obliged," meaning anything the composer views as nonoptional
pizzicato	peets-ee-KAH-toh	"pinched," meaning to pluck the strings rather than bow them; the bowing direction is *arco*.

sostenuto	sohs-teh-NOO-toh	held out or sustained; also the name for the "hold" pedal on a piano
sforzando	sfohr-TSAHN-doh	"forced," meaning strongly accented
staccato	stah-KAH-toh	"detached," meaning that the individual notes are to sound sharply separate; the opposite of *legato*

Finally, a miscellany of terms that are *obbligato* for listening to radio concerts—or at least to the chitchat that follows them:

appogiatura	ah-poh-jah-TOO-rah	a "supporting" note of dissonance that resolves into the harmonic
arpeggio	ahr-PEH-joh	from *arpa*, "harp," a chord played with the notes in sequence rather than all at once
basso continuo or just *continuo*	bah-soh kohn-TEEN-oo-oh	a "continuous" bass line in Baroque music especially
basso ostinato or just *ostinato*	bah-soh aws-tih-NAH-toh	a repeated or "obstinate" bass line
bel canto	behl KAHN-toh	a "beautiful singing" style stressing tone and technique

da capo	dah KAH-poh	"from the head" of a piece of music: a direction to repeat
a capella	ah kah-PEH-lah	in the "church" style, that is, vocally and without instrumentation
divertimento	dih-vehr-tee-MEHN-toh	a humorous musical "diversion"; the French say *divertissement*
intermezzo	ihn-tehr-MEHD-zoh	a comic intermission that was the precursor of *opera buffa*
opera buffa	oh-peh-rah BOO-fah	comic opera; as opposed to *opera seria,* "serious" opera

Fearless Leaders

Pecking orders being what they are throughout the animal kingdom, human beings have concocted a plethora of terms to indicate high social status. The following are some of the more common of these honorific titles:

alcalde
al-KAHL-day
> Spanish: In Moorish Spain a judge; later, and in the New World, a mayor.

archon
AHR-kahn
> Greek: The chief magistrate in ancient Athens. We get "anarchy" from *an-archon,* a period without an *archon.*

bey
bay
> Turkish: "gentleman" or "chief." The ruler of old Tunisia and, more broadly, an Ottoman provincial governor.

Bürgermeister
BUER-ger-MAIS-ter
> German: mayor. Literally "master of the townies."

bwana
BWAH-nuh
> Swahili: boss, master. From the Arabic *abuna,* for "father."

cacique
kah-SEEK
> Spanish: chief, political boss. From the Arawakan originally, it has the sense in Latin America of "strongman." One step up from *jefe.*

capitaine
kah-pee-TAYN
> French: captain, not necessarily as an official rank. The Spanish equivalent is *capitán* (kah-pee-TAHN).

caliph KAY-lihf	Arabic: successor. The successor to Mohammed, and thus the spiritual head of Islam.
capo KA-poh	Italian: chief, and literally "head." Used for traditional clan leaders and modern *mafiosi.*
caudillo kaw-DEE-yoh	Spanish: military dictator. A common title for a Latin American demagogue, it was also adopted by Spain's Francisco Franco, who styled himself *el caudillo.*
commendatore koh-mehn-dah-TAW-ray	Italian: roughly "one who is commended." A common, floating honorific used, social status aside, to show respect.
commissar KAH-mih-sahr	Russian: a (Communist) party leader; originally the head of a state department, now nearly any official.
consul KAHN-suhl	Latin: head of state. Now a diplomatic official, but originally Roman "president." The name means "one who consults."
czar zahr	Russian: head of state before the 1917 Revolution, now a general term for anyone with great power. From the Latin *Caesar.* The feminine form is *czarina* (zahr-EE-nuh).
duce DOO-chay	Italian: leader. From the Latin *dux,* which gives us "duke"; this was the title adopted by Mussolini.
emir AY-meer	Arabic: commander. A ruler in many parts of Asia and Africa.
Führer FUE-rer	German: leader. The title adopted by Adolf Hitler.

generalissimo
jehn-ehr-ahl-EE-see-moh

Spanish: commander-in-chief. Another of Franco's titles, it basically means *"very* general."

guru
GOO-roo

Sanskrit: "heavy." A spiritual teacher or guide.

hetman
HEHT-muhn

Polish: commander-in-chief. An eighteenth-century term for a cossack leader.

hidalgo
ee-DAHL-goh

Spanish: a person of rank. The etymology is from *hijo de algo,* which means basically "son of a somebody."

honcho
HAHN-choh

Japanese: "squad leader," hence any big shot. The Spanish sound is accidental.

jefe
HEH-fay

Spanish: chief, boss, leader. A very loose honorific, implying no particular authority. In the American Southwest, a *jefe* or *jefito* ("little chief") is a father, a *jefa* or *jefita* a mother.

Kaiser
KAI-zer

German: emperor. Like *czar,* from the Latin *Caesar.*

khan
kahn

Turkish: prince. The overlord of Chinese, Mongolian, and other Eastern peoples. the most famous examples are Genghis and Kublai.

maharajah
mah-huh-RAH-juh

Sanskrit: "great *rajah."* The feminine form is *maharani* (mah-huh-RAH-nee)

memsahib
MEHM-sah-eeb

Hindi: mistress. In British movies this sounds like "memsab." It's a fusion of English *ma'am* and Hindi *sahib.*

mikado
mih-KAH-doh

Japanese: emperor. Known to the Western world through the Gilbert and Sullivan opera.

nabob
NAY-bahb

Hindi: from *nawwab,* "governor." Hence anybody of social importance.

padrone
pah-DROH-nay

Italian: master, patron. Similar to the French (and English) *patron* (pah-TRŌH).

rajah
RAH-juh

Hindi: king. Or, more broadly, any princely leader. The feminine version is *rani* (RAH-nee).

sachem
SAY-chuhm

Narragansett: chief, specifically of an Algonquin confederation. Since Tammany times, this has also meant a political boss.

sahib
SAH-eeb

Hindi: master, boss. The standard term of respect from a colonial Indian to a male European overlord. Compare MEMSAHIB.

satrap
SAY-trap

Greek: ruler and more specifically a provincial governor.

sensei
SEHN-say

Japanese: teacher. Given the greater respect afforded authority and knowledge, this is actually closer in connotation to "master."

sharif
shuh-REEF

Arabic: "illustrious." A descendant of Mohammed, and thus someone invested with considerable authority. The similarity to *sheriff* is accidental.

sheikh
shayk

Arabic: chief. The head of a tribal unit, and more generally now—in the Oil Era—any influential Arab leader.

shogun
SHOH-guhn

Japanese: warlord, general. *Shoguns* in effect ruled Japan until the end of the nineteenth century.

vizier
vuh-ZEER

Turkish: *vezir,* an executive officer in old Islam, especially in the Ottoman Empire.

Yiddish Losers

Yiddish has a panoply of terms to describe well-meaning (and some not so well-meaning) losers. Here, with brief notes indebted to Leo Rosten, are a baker's dozen of my favorites:

klutz kluhts	A clumsy or oafish person; a bungler. The *klutz* is always putting his foot in his mouth, or on top of someone's toes.
narr nahr	A fool, a clown. Compare the German word NARRENSCHIFF.
nebbish NEH-bihsh	An ineffectual, unlucky dope; a nobody. Things always happen *to* a *nebbish;* he is "more to be pitied than a SHLEMIHL."
nudnick NOOHD-nihk	A yakky, aggressively boring person; a *nudge.* A *nudnick* with a Ph.D. is a *phudnik.*
putz puhts	A simpleton or jerk. Like SHMUCK, this word also means "penis." *Putz* is the more contemptuous term.
shlemihl shleh-MEEL	The ultimate dope, someone who can do nothing right. Pity the poor *shlemihl:* when he wants to hang himself, he grabs a knife; when he falls on his back, he breaks his nose.
shlimazl shleh-MAH-zl	An unlucky person, a born loser. The term means "bad luck." Like the NEBBISH, the *shlimazl* is the hapless customer on whom the SHLEMIHL waiter spills soup.

shlub shluhb	As clumsy as a KLUTZ, and ill-mannered too. From the Slavic for "coarse."
shmegegge shmeh-GEH-gee	A jerk, but also specifically a sycophant. "The fruit of a NEBBISH and a SHLEMIHL."
shmendrick SHMEHN-drihk	A Caspar Milquetoast, a timid pipsqueak.
shmo shmoh	A euphemism for SHMUCK. Al Capp's "schmoo," who enjoyed being kicked, was a recasting of the *shmo*.
shmuck shmuhk	Slang for "penis," this is also the commonest Yiddishism for "jerk" and for "son of a bitch." Less graphic than PUTZ but almost as insulting.
shnook shnoohk	A pleasant but pathetic sap. *Shnooks* are "more to be pitied than scorned; were they aggressive, they would be SHMUCKS."

Conventional Wisdom

Often a hackneyed saying can take on the ambience of freshness if stated in a *lingua non franca*. To illustrate, here is a gaggle of well-worn proverbs and catchphrases with less familiar foreign equivalents.

Beggars can't be choosers.
>FRENCH: *Faute de grives, on mange des merles.* ("If there aren't any thrushes, one eats blackbirds.")
>FOH duh GREEV ōh māhzh day MEHRL

Better late than never.
>SPANISH: *Más vale tarde que nunca.*
>mahs vah-lay TAHR-day kay NOOHN-kah

Between the Devil and the deep blue sea; between a rock and a hard place; between Scylla and Charybdis.
>SPANISH: *Entre la espada y la pared.* ("Between the sword and the wall.")
>ehn-tray lah ehs-PAH-dah ee lah pah-REHD

Call a spade a spade.
>GREEK: *Ta syka syka, ten skaphen skaphen.* ("Call a fig a fig, a tub a tub.")
>tah SEE-kah SEE-kah, tehn SKAH-fehn SKAH-fehn

Clothes make the man.
>GERMAN: *Kleider machen Leute.*
>KLAI-der makh-ehn LOY-tuh

You can't have your cake and eat it too.
> SPANISH: *No se puede repicar y andar en la procesión.* ("You can't ring the bells and march in the parade.")
> noh say poo-EH-day ray-pee-KAHR ee ahn-dahr ehn lah proh-seh-see-OHN

Cold hands, warm heart.
> GERMAN: *Kalte Hände, warmes Herz.*
> kahl-tuh HEHN-duh, vahr-mehs HEHRTS

In the dark all cats are gray.
> GERMAN: *Bei Nacht sind alle Katzen grau.*
> bai nakht zihnt AH-luh KAHT-zehn grau

Dead men tell no tales.
> FRENCH: *Morte la bête, mort le venin.* ("When the beast is dead, so is the venom.")
> mohrt lah BEHT, mohr luh veh-nēh
> GREEK: *Nekros ou daknei.* ("The dead don't bite.")
> NEH-krohs oo DAHK-nay

Don't speak ill of the dead.
> LATIN: *De mortuis nil nisi bonum.* ("Of the dead say nothing but good.")
> day MOHR-too-ees nihl nee-see BOH-noohm

Each to his own (taste).
> FRENCH: *Chacun à son goût.*
> shah-KŪH ah sōh GOO
> LATIN: *De gustibus non disputandum est.* ("There's no use arguing about taste.")
> day GOOS-tih-boos nohn dihs-poo-TAHN-doohm ehst

The end justifies the means.
> FRENCH: *La fin justifie les moyens.*
> luh FĒH zhoos-tee-fee-AY lay moy-ĒH

To err is human.
> LATIN: *Errare humanum est.*
> ehr-RAH-reh hoo-MAH-noohm ehst

Everything that glitters is not gold.
> GERMAN: *Es ist nicht alles Gold was gläntzt.*
> ehs ihst nihkht AH-lehs gohlt vahs GLEHNST

Faint heart never won fair lady.
> ITALIAN: *Fra Modesto no fu mai priore.* ("Brother Modest won't become prior.")
> frah moh-DEHS-toh noh foo mai pree-AW-ray

Fate will find a way.
> LATIN: *Fata viam invenient.*
> FAH-tah WEE-ahm ihn-WEH-nee-ehnt

Fortune favors the bold.
> LATIN: *Audaces fortuna juvat.*
> au-DAH-kehs fawr-TOO-nah YOO-waht

The fruit doesn't fall far from the tree.
> GREEK: *Kakou korakos kakon oon.* ("From a bad crow, a bad egg.")
> KAH-koo KOH-rah-kohs KAH-kohn oh-ohn

Heaven helps those who help themselves.
> FRENCH: *Aide-toi, le ciel t'aidera.*
> ayd TWAH, luh see-ehl tay-deh-RAH
> GERMAN: *Hilf dir selbst, so hilft dir Gott.*
> hihlf deer ZEHLPST, zoh hihlft deer GAWT

If the shoe fits, wear it.
> SPANISH: *Si te cae el saco, póntelo.* ("If a dress falls on you, put it on.")
> see tay kai ehl SAH-koh, POHN-teh-loh

Ignorance of the law is no excuse.
> LATIN: *Ignorantia juris non excusat.*
> ihg-noh-RAHN-tee-ah YOO-rihs nohn ehx-KOO-zaht

In the land of the blind, the one-eyed man is king.
    FRENCH: *Au royaume des aveugles les borgnes sont rois.*
      oh roy-OHM dayz-ah-VEUHGL lay BOHRN sōh RWAH
    SPANISH: *En tierra de ciegos, el tuerto es rey.*
      ehn tee-EH-rah day see-AY-gohs, ehl too-EHR-toh ehs ray

Let the buyer beware.
    LATIN: *Caveat emptor.*
      KAH-vay-aht EHMP-tawr

Lie down with dogs, wake up with fleas.
    SPANISH: *Si duermes con los perros te levantas con pulgas.*
      see doo-EHR-mehs kohn lohs PEHR-rohs, tay lay-VAHN-tahs kohn
      POOL-gahs

Life is a dream.
    GERMAN: *Der Traum ein Leben.*
      dehr TRAUM ain LAY-behn
    SPANISH: *La vida es sueño.*
      lah VEE-dah ehs SWAY-nyoh

Love conquers all.
    LATIN: *Amor vincit omnia.*
      AH-mawr WIHN-kiht AWM-nee-ah

Love is blind.
    SPANISH: *El amor es ciego.*
      ehl ah-MOHR ehs see-AY-goh

Man proposes, God disposes.
    FRENCH: *L'homme propose, Dieu dispose.*
      luhm proh-POHZ, dee-UE dihs-POHZ

A man's home is his castle.
    GERMAN: *Jeder ist Kaiser in seine Lage.* ("Everyone's an emperor in
    his own place.")
      YAY-der ihst KAI-zer ihn ZAI-nuh LAH-guh

There's many a slip 'twixt the cup and the lip.
> SPANISH: *Del plato a la boca se pierde la sopa.* ("Between the plate and the mouth, the soup falls.")
> dehl PLAH-toh ah lah BOH-kah say pee-EHR-day lah SOH-pah

A mountain out of a molehill.
> RUSSIAN: *Delat iz mukhi slona.* ("Make an elephant out of a fly.")
> DAY-laht ihz MOO-kee SLOH-nah

No news is good news.
> ITALIAN: *Nulla nuova, buona nuova.*
> NOOH-lah noo-OH-vah, boo-OH-nah noo-OH-vah

One day at a time.
> SPANISH: *Gota a gota el mar se apoca.* ("The sea is emptied drop by drop.")
> GOH-tah ah GOH-tah ehl MAHR say ah-POH-kah

One good turn deserves another.
> GERMAN: *Eine Hand wäscht die andere.* ("One hand washes the other.")
> AI-nuh hahnt vehsh dee AHN-deh-ruh
> SPANISH: *Amor con amor se paga.* ("Love is repaid with love.")
> AH-mohr kohn AH-mohr say PAH-gah

Out of sight, out of mind.
> GREEK: *Aisoi, apustoi.*
> AI-soy, ah-POOHS-toy
> SPANISH: *Santo que no es visto no es adorado.* ("The unseen saint is not adored.")
> SAHN-toh kay noh ehs VEES-toh noh ehs ah-doh-RAH-doh

The pot calling the kettle black.
> SPANISH: *Dijo la sartén a la caldera: 'Quítate, culinegra!'* ("The frying pan said to the kettle, 'Get away, black bottom!' ")
> DEE-hoh lah sahr-TEHN ah lah kahl-DAY-rah: KEE-tah-tay, koo-lee-NAY-grah

Practice makes perfect.
GERMAN: *Übung macht den Meister.* ("Practice makes the master.")
UE-boohng mahkht dehn MAIS-ter

Pride goes before a fall.
SWAHILI: *Alioko juu, mngoje chini* ("Wait below for the one above.")
ah-lee-oh-koh joo mn-goh-jeh chee-nee

A rolling stone gathers no moss.
FRENCH: *Pierre qui roule n'amasse pas mousse.*
pee-EHR kee rool nah-MAHS pah MOOS

There's no place like home.
GREEK: *Hos ouden glukion hes patridos.* ("No place is sweeter than
one's native land.")
hohs OO-dehn GLOO-kee-ohn hehs PAH-tree-dohs

There's the rub (heart of the matter).
GERMAN: *Da liegt der Hund begraben.*
dah leekt der hoohnt beh-GRAH-behn
RUSSIAN: *Vot gde sobaka zaryta.*
voht gday soh-BAHK-ah zah-REE-tah
(Both the German and the Russian expressions mean "That's
where the dog is buried.")

Time is money.
GERMAN: *Zeit ist teuer.* ("Time is expensive.")
tsait ihst TOY-er

Don't trust to luck.
GERMAN: *Glück und Glas, wie bald bricht das.* ("Luck and glass are
soon broken.")
gluek oohnt glahs, vee bahlt brihkht dahs

What will be, will be.
ITALIAN: *Che sarà sarà.*
kay sah-RAH sah-RAH

When the cat's away the mice will play.
    SPANISH: *Cuando el gato va a sus devociones, bailan las ratones.*
    ("When the cat goes to pray, the mice dance.")
    kwahn-doh ehl GAH-toh vah ah soo day-voh-see-OH-nays, BAI-yahn lahs rah-TOH-nays

While there's life there's hope.
    LATIN: *Dum spiro spero.* ("While I breathe, I hope.")
    doohm SPEE-roh SPEH-roh

Where there's smoke there's fire.
    LATIN: *Flamma fumo est proxima.* ("Flame is near to smoke.")
    FLAH-mah FOO-moh ehst PRAWX-ih-mah

Where there's a will there's a way.
    FRENCH: *Celui qui veut, peut.*
    seh-lwee kee veu, peu

He won't set the world on fire.
    RUSSIAN: *Porokhu ne vydumayet.* ("He won't invent gunpowder.")
    poh-ROH-koo nay VYIH-doo-MAI-eht

You've made your bed, now lie in it.
    GERMAN: *Wie man sich bettet, so schläft man.* ("You sleep as you make your bed.")
    vee mahn zihkh BEH-teht, zoh shlehft mahn

Toasts

Drinking "healths" with friends is an ancient custom that has survived in most cultures. Even people in Muslim countries drink toasts, although they usually do so with nonalcoholic beverages. Robert Garrison's charming compilation *Here's to You* gives scores of examples from around the world. Here is a modest selection.

Language	Toast	Meaning
Arabic	kah-sahk	Your cup
	soo-khah-tahk	Your health
Chinese	gahn bay*	Dry the cup
Czech	*Na zdrávi*	Health
	(NAHZ-drah-vee)	
Dutch	*Proost* †	May it benefit
	(prohst)	
French	*À votre santé*	To your health
	(ah VOH-truh SÃH-tay)	
German	*Prosit* †	May it benefit
	(PROH-ziht)	
Greek	see-EE-ah	Health
Hebrew/Yiddish	l'KHAIM	To life
Hungarian	*Egeszsegedre*	Health
	(eh-geh-SHEE-geh-dreh)	
Irish/Scottish	*Slainthe*	Health
	(SLAHN-cheh)	

Language	Toast	Meaning
Italian	*Alla tua salute* (ah-lah TOO-ah sah-LOO-tay)	To your health
	Cin cin ‡ (CHIHN chihn)	
Japanese	kahn pai*	Drink
Korean	goohn bai*	Drink
Polish	*Na zdrowie* (nahz-DROH-vyeh)	Health
Portuguese	*À sua saúde* (ah SOO-ah sah-OO-deh)	To your health
Russian	nahz-dah-ROH-vyih	Health
Scandinavian§	*Skål* (skohl)	Cup, bowl
Spanish	*Salud* (sah-LOOD)	Health
Swahili	AHF-yah YAH-koh	Your health
Vietnamese	shuek bahn nee-oo shue-kway	Health to you, friend
Yugoslav (Serbo-Croatian)	*Ziveli/Zivile* (masc./fem.) (ZHEE-veh-lee/ZHEE-vih-leh)	To life

---

*The Japanese and Korean common toasts, with slightly different pronunciations, are taken from the Chinese.

†Dutch *proost* and German *prosit* are "mock-Deutsch" adaptations of the Latin *prosit.*

‡*Cin cin* is a variant of an old Chinese good luck wish, brought to Europe by Italian traders.

§Scandinavian of course is not a language, but *skål* is a universal toast in the Scandinavian countries—Denmark, Finland, Iceland, Norway, and Sweden. In the last it is spelled *skäl.*

Common Abbreviations of Foreign Terms

Abbreviation	Term	Meaning
A.D.	LATIN: *anno domini*	in the year of our lord
aet.	LATIN: *aetatis suae; aetatis*	in the year of his/her age; aged
A.M.	LATIN: *ante meridiem*	before noon
c. or ca.	LATIN: *circa*	about, approximately
cantab.	LATIN: *cantabrigiensis*	of Cambridge
cf.	LATIN: *confer*	compare
d.c.	ITALIAN: *da capo*	from the head (music)
d.s.	ITALIAN: *dal segno*	from the sign (music)
DTs	LATIN: *delirium tremens*	delirium tremens
e.g.	LATIN: *exempli gratia*	for example
et al.	LATIN: *et alii*	and others
etc.	LATIN: *et cetera*	and so forth
et seq.	LATIN: *et sequens*	and the following
ibid.	LATIN: *ibidem*	in the same place
id.	LATIN: *idem*	the same
i.e.	LATIN: *id est*	that is
IHS	GREEK: *Iesus*	Jesus

(often erroneously thought to stand for Latin *Iesus hominum salvator,* "Jesus the savior of mankind")

I.N.R.I.	LATIN: *Iesus Nazarenus Rex Iudaeorum*	Jesus of Nazareth, King of the Jews
lb.	LATIN: *libra*	pound
loc. cit.	LATIN: *loco citato*	in the place cited
n.	LATIN: *natus*	born
N.B.	LATIN: *nota bene*	note well

Abbreviation	Term	Meaning
ob.	LATIN: *obiit*	he/she died
op. cit.	LATIN: *opere citato*	in the work cited
oxon.	LATIN: *oxoniensis*	from Oxford
P.M.	LATIN: *post meridiem*	after noon
pro tem.	LATIN: *pro tempore*	temporary
P.S.	LATIN: *postscriptum*	postscript
Q.E.D.	LATIN: *quod erat demonstrandum*	that which was to be demonstrated
q.v.	LATIN: *quod vide*	which see (refer to)
R.I.P.	LATIN: *requiescat in pace*	rest in peace
R.S.V.P.	FRENCH: *répondez s'il vous plaît*	please reply
S.P.Q.R.	LATIN: *Senatus populusque romanus*	the Senate and the Roman people
sup.	LATIN: *supra*	above
u.s.w.	GERMAN: *und so weiter*	and so on
v.	LATIN: *vide*	see (refer to)

Common Phrases

ARABIC

Hello	*mahr-khah-bahn*
How are you?	*kayf al-hahl* ("How is the state of things?")
Fine/OK	*hih-khayr al khahm-doo lih-lah* ("In goodness, praise be to God")
Yes	*nah-ahm*
No	*lah*
Excuse me	*ahf-wahn*
Please	*mihn fahd-lahk/mihn fahd-lihk* (masc./fem.)
Thank you	*shoo-krahn*
You're welcome	*ahf-wahn*
Goodbye	*mah-ah-sah-lah-mah* ("With safety")

CHINESE

Hello	*nee hau mah* ("Are you well?")
How are you?	*tseh-mah-yahng* ("How goes it?")
Fine/OK	*hau*
Yes	*dway* ("You're right")
	shr ("It is")
No	*boo-dway* ("You're not right")
	boo-shr ("It is not")
Excuse me	*dway-boo-chee*
Please	*chihng*
Thank you	*syeh syeh*
You're welcome	*boo syeh*
Goodbye	*tsai chyehn*

FRENCH

Hello	Bonjour ("Good day")	*bōh ZHOOR*
	Bonsoir ("Good evening")	*bōh SWAHR*
How are you?	Comment allez-vous?	*kaw-MÃH tah-lay-VOO*
	Comment ça va?	*kaw-MÃH sah VAH*
Fine/OK	Bien	*byēh*
	Ça va	*sah VAH*
Yes	Oui	*wee*
No	Non	*nōh*
Excuse me	Excusez-moi	*ehks-KUE-zay MWAH*
	Pardonnez-moi	*pahr-DAW-nay MWAH*
	Pardon	*pahr-DÃW*
Please	S'il vous plaît	*seel voo PLEH*
Thank you	Merci	*mehr-SEE*
You're welcome	Pas de quoi	*PAH duh KWAH*
Goodbye	Au revoir	*oh ruh-VWAHR*
	À bientôt	*ah byehn TOH*

GERMAN

Hello	Guten Morgen ("Good morning")	*GOO-tehn MAWR-gehn*
	Guten Tag ("Good day")	*GOO-tehn TAHK*
	Guten Abend ("Good evening")	*GOO-tehn AH-behnt*
	Gute Nacht ("Good night")	*GOO-tuh NAKHT*
How are you?	Wie geht es Ihnen?	*vee GAYT ehs EE-nehn*
	Wie geht's?	*vee GAYTS*
Fine/OK, and you?	Gut, und Ihnen?	*GOOT, oohnt EE-nehn*

Yes	Ja	*yah*
No	Nein	*nain*
Excuse me	Entschuldigen Sie mir	*ehnt-SHOOL-dih-gehn zee MEER*
	Verzeihen Sie mir	*fehr-TSAI-ehn zee MEER*
Please	Bitte	*BIH-tuh*
Thank you	Danke (schön)	*DAHN-kuh (shoen)*
You're welcome	Bitte schön	*BIH-tuh shoen*
Goodbye	Auf Wiedersehen	*auf VEE der..ayn*

ITALIAN

Hello	Buon giorno ("Good day")	*bwawn JOHR-noh*
	Buona sera ("Good evening")	*bwaw-nah SAY-rah*
	Buona notte ("Good night")	*bwaw-nah NAW-teh*
How are you?	Come sta?	*KOH-may STAH*
Fine/OK	Bene	*BEH-nay*
Yes	Sì	*see*
No	No	*naw*
Excuse me	Scusi	*SKOO-see*
Please	Per favore	*payr fah-VOH-reh*
	Per piaccre	*payr pyah-CHAY-reh*
Thank you	Grazie	*GRAH-tsyeh*
You're welcome	Prego	*PREH-goh*
Goodbye	Arrivederci	*ah-ree-veh-DAYR-chee*
	Ciao	*chau*

JAPANESE

Hello	*oh-hi-oh* ("Good morning")
	koh-nih-chee wah ("Good day")
	kohm-bah wah ("Good evening")
How are you?	*oh-gehn-kih-deh-soo-kah*
Fine/OK	*gehn-kih-deh-soo ah-nah-tah-wah*

Yes	*hai*
No	*ee-eh*
Excuse me	*shih-tsoo-reh-shih-mah-soo*
Please	*doh-zoh*
	koo-dah-sai
Thank you	*ah-ree-gah-toh go-zai-mahs*
You're welcome	*doh ee tah shih-mah shih-teh*
Goodbye	*sah-yoh-nah-rah*

PORTUGUESE

Hello	Ola ("Hello")	*oh-LAH*
	Bom dia ("Good day")	*bōh DEE-uh*
	Boa tarde ("Good afternoon")	*boh-ah TAHR-duh*
	Boa noite ("Good evening")	*boh-ah NOY-tuh*
How are you?	Como vai?	*KOH-moo VAI*
Fine/OK	Muito bem	*moo-ee-too BĒH*
Yes	Sim	*sēe*
No	Não	*nāu*
Excuse me	Desculpe	*desh-KOOL-pay*
	Com licença	*kōh lee-SĒH-sah*
Please	Por favor	*poor fah-VOOR*
	Faz favor	*fash fah-VOOR*
	Faça favor	*fah-sah fah-VOOR*
Thank you	Obrigado (masc.)	*oo-bree-GAH-doo*
	Obrigada (fem.)	*oo-bree-GAH-duh*
You're welcome	De nada	*duh NAH-duh*
Goodbye	Adeus	*ah-DEH-oosh*
	Tchau*	*chau*

*Adapted from the Italian *Ciao*.

RUSSIAN

Hello	*DAW-bruh-yeh OO-truh* ("Good morning")
	DAW-brih VYEH-chihr ("Good evening")
	DAW-brih dehn ("Good day")
How are you?	*kahk pah-zhih-VAH-yih-tyih*
Fine/OK	*khah-rah-SHOH*
Yes	*dah*
No	*nyeht*
Excuse me	*ihz-vih-NYEE-tyih*
Please	*pah-ZHAHL-stuh*
Thank you	*spah-SYIH-buh* ("God save")
You're welcome	*NEH zuh shtuh* ("Not for what")
Goodbye	*dah svih-DAHN-yuh*

SPANISH

Hello	Hola ("Hello")	*OH-lah*
	Buenos días ("Good day")	*BWEH-nohs DEE-ahs*
	Buenas tardes ("Good afternoon")	*BWEH-nahs TAHR-dehs*
	Buenas noches ("Good evening")	*BWEH-nahs NOH-chehs*
How are you?	¿Cómo está usted?	*KOH-moh ehs-TAH oos-TEHD*
Fine/OK	Muy bien	*mwee BYEHN*
Yes	Sí	*see*
No	No	*noh*
Excuse me	Perdóneme	*pehr-DOH-nah-may*
	Dispénsame	*dee-SPEHN-sah-may*
Please	Por favor	*pohr fah-VOHR*
Thank you	Gracias	*GRAH-see-ahs*
You're welcome	De nada	*day NAH-dah*
Goodbye	Adiós	*ah-DYOHS*
	Hasta la vista	*AHS-tah lah VEES-tah*
	Hasta luego	*AHS-tah LWEH-goh*

SWAHILI

Hello	*JAHM-boh*
How are you?	*hah-BAH-ree GAH-nee?*
Fine/OK	*n'ZOO-ree SAH-nah*
	n'JEH-mah
Yes	*n'DEE-oh*
No	*hah-PAH-nah*
Excuse me	*SAH-mah-HAH-nee*
Please	*tah-fah-DAH-lee*
Thank you	*ah-SAHN-teh*
You're welcome	*ah-SAHN-teh*
Goodbye	*kwah-HEH-ree*

YIDDISH

Hello	*SHOH-lehm ah-LAY-khehm* ("Peace be with you")
How are you?	*vohs MAHKHS too?* ("What are you doing?")
Fine/OK	*gooht*
Yes	*yoh*
No	*nayn*
Excuse me	*zai MOY-kh'l* ("Be forgiving")
Please	*zai ah-ZOY gooht* ("Be so good")
Thank you	*AH-dahnk*
You're welcome	*NEE-toh sahr vohs* ("For nothing")
Goodbye	*ZAI geh-ZOOHNT* ("Be well")

Bibliography

Ammer, Christine. *Harper's Dictionary of Music.* New York: Barnes and Noble, 1973.

Anderson, Beatrix, and Maurice North. *Beyond the Dictionary in German.* New York: Funk & Wagnalls, 1969.

Beaudoin, John, and Everett Mattlin. *The Phrase-Dropper's Handbook.* New York: Dell, 1976.

Benét, William Rose. *The Reader's Encyclopedia.* New York: Thomas Y. Crowell, 1965.

Bentley, Harold W. *A Dictionary of Spanish Terms in English.* New York: Columbia University Press, 1932.

Brewer, E. Cobham. *Brewer's Dictionary of Phrase and Fable.* Edited by Ivor Evans. New York: Harper & Row, 1981.

Buchanan-Brown, John, et al., eds. *Le Mot Juste: A Dictionary of Classical & Foreign Words and Phrases.* New York: Vintage, 1981.

Collison, Robert and Mary, eds. *Dictionary of Foreign Quotations.* New York: Everest House, 1980.

Dubrovin, M. I. *A Book of Russian Idioms Illustrated.* Moscow: Russian Language Publishers, 1980.

Ehrlich, Eugene. *Amo, Amas, Amat and More.* New York: Harper & Row, 1985.

Geneviève. *Merde Encore!* New York: Atheneum, 1987.

Gerrard, A. Bryson, and José de Heras Heras. *Beyond the Dictionary in Spanish.* New York: Funk & Wagnalls, 1964.

Glendening, P. J. T. *Beyond the Dictionary in Italian.* New York: Funk & Wagnalls, 1964.

Levieux, Michel and Eleanor. *Beyond the Dictionary in French.* New York: Funk & Wagnalls, 1967.

Newmark, Maxim. *Dictionary of Foreign Words and Phrases.* Philosophical Library, repr. 1986 (1950).

Oxford University Press Dictionary of Quotations. 2nd edition. New York: Crescent Books, 1985.

Pei, Mario. *Talking Your Way Around the World.* 2nd edition. New York: Harper & Row, 1967.

Rogers, James. *The Dictionary of Clichés.* New York: Facts on File, 1985.

Rosten, Leo. *Hooray for Yiddish.* New York: Simon and Schuster, 1982.

———. *The Joys of Yiddish.* New York: McGraw-Hill, 1968.

Vasquez, Librado Keno and Maria Enriqueta. *Regional Dictionary of Chicano Slang.* Austin, Texas: Jenkins Publishing Company, 1975.

Woodward, Ian. *Ballet.* Sevenoaks, Kent: Hodder and Stoughton, 1977.

Index of Foreign Words and Phrases

This index includes all foreignisms *not* listed alphabetically in the body of the book.

179

Subject Index

This index contains two kinds of main entry. First, there are English translations of foreign phrases familiar as common expressions in English. Second, there are subject categories, like those of a thesaurus, to help you find *le mot juste* for any occasion.

Abandon hope, all who enter here, 74
abbreviations (See also COMMON
    ABBREVIATIONS, 169–170)
  A.A.S., 9
  ad inf., 6
  ad lib., 7
  A.M.D.G., 7
  A.S., 9
  AUC, 135
  d. aet., 9
  DCCAUC, 135
  M.O., 83
  ob. aet., 9
academia
  ad eundem gradum, 5–6
  alma mater, 11
  cantabrigiensis (cantab.), 169
  oxoniensis (oxon.), 170
  Wanderjahre, 129
act of faith, 20
act of God, 4
aesthetics
  bella, 23
  bella figura, 23
  bellissima, 23
  brutta figura, 23–24
  che bella, 23
  Schönheit, 111
affectation
  ex libris, 50
  les cinq lettres, 33
  préciosité, x
  qua, 101

  quae cum ita sint, 101
  recherché, 106
  soi-disant, 116
affirmation
  Ça marche, 30
  Ça va, 30, 172
  Ça va sans dire, 30
  claro, 33
  con mucho gusto, 35
  d'accord, 38–39
  mazel tov, 79
  pace tua, 93
  schön, 111
After us, the deluge, 15
against the grain, 16
a healthy mind in a healthy body, 81
all for one, one for all, 121
always faithful, 111
always prepared, 111
A man's home is his castle, 163
amazing to say, 82
A mountain out of a molehill, 164
anatomy
  kishke(s), 71
  nez retroussé, 106
  pupik, 101
  retroussé, 106
  tuches, 123
  tush, 123
an embarrassment of riches, 46
an empty slate, 118
animation
  carpe diem, 29